How to Beat

Worry and Generalised Anxiety Disorder

One Step at a Time

Marie Chellingsworth
and Paul Farrand

ROBINSON

ROBINSON

First published in Great Britain in 2016 by Robinson

Important Note
This book is not intended as a substitute for medical advice
or treatment. Any person with a condition requiring medical
attention should consult a qualified medical practitioner or
suitable therapist.

A CIP catalogue record for this book
is available from the British Library.

ISBN 978-1-47210-885-2 (paperback)

Typeset in Minion by Initial Typesetting Services, Edinburgh
Printed and bound in Great Britain by Clays Ltd, St Ives plc

Papers used by Robinson are from well-managed forests
and other responsible sources

MIX
Paper from
responsible sources
FSC® C104740
www.fsc.org

Robinson
is an imprint of
Little, Brown Book Group
Carmelite House
50 Victoria Embankment
London EC4Y 0DZ

An Hachette UK Company
www.hachette.co.uk

www.littlebrown.co.uk

CONTENTS

Section 1: Getting going   1

Section 2: Understanding Generalised Anxiety
    Disorder (GAD) and the role of worry   23

Section 3: Managing your worry   46

Section 4: Managing the future   96

Section 5: Graham and Sarah's stories   121

Further resources   153

Dedications and acknowledgements   241

Index   243

GETTING GOING

Nice to meet you!

We are really glad that you have started reading this book and we hope that you will find it useful. This book is designed as a guide to teach you a range of techniques that you can put into action if you experience excessive or uncontrollable worrying. If your worry is impacting on your life, these techniques can help you to help yourself feel better. It may be that a healthcare practitioner has told you that you have symptoms indicative of Generalised Anxiety Disorder (GAD) so you want to find out more and see what can be done to help. We have made sure the book contains useful information; as well as evidence-based techniques that can help with the symptoms you are experiencing. It is based upon Cognitive Behavioural Therapy (CBT), an evidence-based form of psychological therapy. CBT is the treatment of choice for people with GAD recommended by the National Institute of Health and

Care Excellence (NICE). This recommendation is because there are a significant number of research trials that have shown CBT to be effective for people who are experiencing GAD. In addition, we can personally recommend CBT based on our own clinical practice. We will explain more about CBT and how it works later in this section.

The techniques this book contains have helped many people with GAD to feel better. We hope the techniques will benefit you too. An important part of that is learning to manage your worry and anxiety more effectively so that you can feel in control of it rather than it feeling like it is controlling you. This guide will form your own personal toolkit. By working through it and putting it into action, it will provide you with a range of ways to feel more in control and manage how you are feeling.

We have written this book in short sections so that you can work through it at a pace that suits you. We have also included examples of other people with worry and GAD who have used the various techniques themselves. These recovery stories show how they put the techniques into action in their daily lives to improve how they were feeling. They have also provided us with some top tips to share with you.

They are honest accounts that show there are things you can do that will help you to manage your worry.

It is not always easy, and there is no quick fix, but by putting these techniques into action in your every-day life, small changes lead to bigger change.

We hope you find this book useful and we will be with you as you work through it to motivate and support you.

Getting to know us

First of all, we would like to introduce ourselves. Below, we will tell you a little about who we are and why we have written this book. We both work clini-cally with patients with depression and anxiety dis-orders using Cognitive Behavioural Therapy (CBT). CBT is recommended for people with low mood, depression and anxiety and is the approach used in this book. We have taught many other practitioners to use CBT to help other people on the training courses we have run. We have both worked with the Department of Health and other organisations to help set standards for training and delivery of CBT in England.

Marie Chellingsworth: I am Executive Director of CBT and Evidence-Based Interventions in the Department of Clinical Psychology, at UEA Medical School. Prior to this, I led training programmes for Psychological Wellbeing Practitioners (PWPs) and undergraduate Applied Psychology (Clinical) students whilst Programme Director at the universities of Nottingham and then Exeter. I am passionate about CBT training and ensuring people over the age of 65 get equal access to treatment. Clinically, my interest areas are GAD, depression and other anxiety problems. I have a particular interest in dementia; and working with carers and those over 65. I am currently renovating an old lodge house in the countryside in Devon that I share with my Irish setters Alfie and Monty and cat called Hendrix (named after the one and only Jimi). I love good music, interior design and spending time with friends. My secret pleasure though is watching *Emmerdale*!

Paul Farrand: I am an Associate Professor and health psychologist. Clinically, most of my work has been with people with physical health problems and depression. Most recently I worked with people in hospital with head, neck and jaw problems. My recent research focus is developing CBT self-help for armed forces veterans. Outside of work I enjoy spending time with my wife, Paula, and our three children, Oliver, Ellis and Amélie. We enjoy eating out and long walks in the East Devon countryside and coastline with our two black Labradors. I also have an interest in 1950s British cinema.

Using this book

This book uses a self-help approach. It guides you through CBT techniques that you can put into practice at a pace and at a time that suits you. You also have the book to always be able to refer back to. You are in charge of how and when you use it. To get the most from it, the key thing is to put it into action in your daily life. To support you to do this, we have broken the book down into short sections and made it a small pocket-book size. You can carry the book around with you so that you have the techniques and worksheets close at hand whenever you need to go through them or are doing an activity.

Sections of the book

The book is divided into five sections; here is an overview so that you can see where things are:

Section 1: Getting going

In this section we will look at where to start in using the book and how to get the maximum benefit from it. There are also resources to help you to set goals to monitor your progress as well as techniques that you can use at the start or at any time if you struggle with motivation to keep going.

Section 2: Understanding worry and Generalised Anxiety Disorder (GAD)

We begin by looking at Generalised Anxiety Disorder (GAD), what maintains it and how it can be treated. There are top tips for getting started from other people who have used these techniques themselves to help with their GAD and from trained practitioners who support people with GAD to feel better. We will help you to understand more about how your anxiety is affecting you and what may be maintaining it. We will then introduce the CBT techniques that can help you to manage those symptoms, and show you how they work.

Section 3: Techniques to put into action to improve how you feel

In Section 3 we help you to make your own plan for feeling better by using the CBT techniques. You will learn how to classify different types of worries and learn effective strategies to help you to control your worries and symptoms of anxiety more effectively. There are four techniques that you can choose from and use to target the things you have identified as affecting you in particular. You can then put your plan into action and review your progress.

Section 4: Relapse prevention

Section 4 helps you make a plan for managing your anxiety and worry in the future and staying well. It helps you to spot your early warning signs that things may be going off track. It helps you to get things going in the right direction again.

Section 5: Sarah and Graham's recovery stories

In Section 5 you can hear more from Sarah and Graham, who have used these techniques to help with their own difficulties. You will first meet them briefly in Section 2, where they introduce themselves. In Section 5 you can see what they did and how they did it, as well as looking at the techniques they used and seeing some examples of their own completed worksheets. They have shared their own stories of having Generalised Anxiety Disorder and what helped them. We know that people find it valuable to see how other people have put things into action to feel better. Their stories may be different from your own situation, but the techniques they have used are the ones that are recommended to help you with your own worry and anxiety.

Where to start?

We have tried to make using this book as easy as possible for you by breaking it into sections and steps. Getting started can be the hardest step, so by reading this far, you are already making progress towards feeling better. Keep up the great work! Some people like to read through everything first and then start to use the techniques themselves. Others prefer to hear from other people who have used the techniques first and some may just want to get going. Anywhere you choose to start is fine. All we would ask is that you set some goals in this section before you put your plan into action. Goals help to motivate you to keep going, help you to monitor your progress, and ensure that your plan is focused on where you want to be, is specific, measurable and achievable.

The important thing is that wherever you do choose to start reading, you also make a conscious choice to keep going and to put the techniques into practice in your daily life. Work through the techniques at a pace that suits you and complete the activities as you go along. Where and how you start is entirely up to you. Remember, this is an interactive self-help guide! You will get the most from it by putting it into action.

If you want to read about other people who have experienced worry and Generalised Anxiety Disorder and how this approach has helped them, in Section 5 we have included two recovery stories of Sarah and Graham who have kindly shared their stories and what they did to manage their worry and anxiety.

Support to use it

It may be that your healthcare practitioner recommended this self-help book and you will be using it together. If that is the case, they can answer any questions you may have and help you along the way too. It may be that you are already receiving support from a GP or other healthcare practitioner. In England, Australia, and spreading to other countries because of their success, there are free Improving Access to Psychological Therapies (IAPT) services. They provide support sessions, face-to-face or over the phone, with a Psychological Wellbeing Practitioner (PWP) or coach. These people are specialist mental health practitioners who support you to work through CBT self-help techniques like the ones in this book. If you are receiving support, it is likely that you will speak to them regularly either face-to-face or over the telephone. They will help you to identify and solve any problems you have putting the techniques into action and answer any questions you may have. The focus is on working together, rather than them simply telling you what you should do. There is work for you between sessions to put into practice the techniques and skills that you learn. They will go at the pace you want to go and really put you in control.

Tell whoever is providing the support that you are using this book, so their support can be tailored to it.

Remember you are the expert in how you are feeling and your own situation. The person who is supporting you has expertise in the techniques and in supporting and encouraging people to use them. There can be a short waiting time to see someone but they aim to see people as quickly as possible and services are monitored to ensure they offer timely access. In England, to find out about your local service, go to:

http://www.iapt.nhs.uk/services/ www.

or

http://www.nhs.uk/Service-Search/Psycho logicaltherapyNHSIAPTLocationSearch /396 www.

You may wish to work through this book alone or with a friend or family member. Research has shown that people can use CBT approaches without support and get benefit from them. Equally, we know that getting support can keep people motivated and help them to get the most from this type of approach. If you think that would help you, you can find out more about what may be available through your GP or healthcare provider. If you are working through it alone, or with a friend or family member, making notes and using Post-it notes to mark key pages can help you to keep up your progress. Write reminders in your calendar or phone to remind you to use the approach. If motivation is a problem for you, don't forget you can use the techniques below to help you with that at any time.

You may not be receiving support to use this book, but would like to, or you may live in an area where IAPT or similar services are not yet available. You can work through it independently and put the techniques into action, but if you feel that you would benefit from the support of someone to motivate and encourage you to use it you can talk to your GP. He or she may have access to other services that can offer support in your local area or who can recommend a service or an accredited CBT therapist.

Please write in the book!

You may, like us, have been told not to write in your books when you were younger. However, books like this are different – they are interactive and designed to be written in! People using CBT-based approaches have told us that highlighting bits that they found helpful or had questions about or making notes in the book as they went along can be really beneficial. There are worksheets in the book specifically designed for you to complete. Please do write in it as much and as often as you want to. You can also write down questions you may want to ask your GP or other healthcare practitioner who is supporting you. The techniques in this book rely on having the worksheets completed as a record of your progress and to monitor change. We cannot stress how important completing them is! Other people have told us this is really helpful too. Remember if at any time you are not sure about something, you can come back to the book and look at that part again and you will have your notes to look back on too!

Each time there is something for you to write in and complete, you will see this sign:

Building motivation to change

It can be difficult getting going at first. You may be pulled between feeling that your worry and anxiety is out of control and also not wanting to stop worrying in case you are unprepared, or something goes wrong. That in itself is a common worry for people with GAD when starting out on the path to feeling better. It can be hard for anyone to make changes and set time aside to do it, but when you have worried for a long time, it can be hard to imagine what your life will be like without worry.

Change is hard for all of us. Think back to the last time you learned a new skill or hobby. Did you feel motivated all the time? Or did it come and go? What made you stick with it? Is there anything that you have learned from things you have done in the past, or changes you have made that you can use to help you with this book?

People using CBT approaches and practitioners supporting them have found that using motivation techniques like the ones below can be helpful. They give you the space to think about the benefits of making changes using the techniques and the positive impact that this can have on your life.

If you feel this would be helpful for you, then complete the boxes below. These exercises will help you to think about what your life will be like again without worrying excessively and having high levels of anxiety. What would you be doing differently as a result? What benefits would there be? You can write as much or as little as you like.

Building motivation to change exercises

1. Imagine for a few minutes that you decide not to make any changes and that your life carries on the way it is now. You still worry a lot and find it impacts on your life. You may avoid things as a result of your worries and anxiety. Things may keep going in the same way they are now or may get worse. If things carried on like this, how would you feel? What would your life be like? What would you be missing out on as a result or not doing that you would like to be doing?

2. Then visualise what would your life be like in five years if you make changes and feel better? How would you know you were feeling better? If someone could wave a magic wand and take all of your symptoms away, what would it be like for you? What would you be doing differently as a result? What would you like to do that you are not currently doing?

Setting goals

Above, you have thought about what your life would be like in five years' time with your worries and anxiety back to a manageable level. You have also visualised what life could be like when you feel better. Now we would like you to think about getting there and achieving the life you want.

What would you like to achieve over the next few weeks and months in using this guide? Setting some goals can help you to measure your progress and keep you feeling motivated. These may be goals to get back to doing things you have done in the past, or even entirely new things you would like to do. Try and make these goals things that are specific to you, things that you can measure your progress against, and that are realistic for you to achieve.

The easiest way to think about a goal is to think what you would be doing if you felt better. If those symptoms you currently experience had gone, where would you be going? What would you be doing differently and what would life be like then? Try and break these things down into stages. What steps can you take towards the goal you want to achieve in the short, medium and longer term? First, come up with two or three bigger goals you would like to achieve. Then you can think about things in the short, medium and longer term that you can do towards achieving them, to break those goals down.

My goals for feeling better

Goal 1:...

Longer term things I can do to work towards this goal over the next six months or so.

_____

_____

Things that I can do towards this goal in the next month.

_____

_____

Things I can do towards this goal in the next couple of weeks.

_____

Goal 2: ....

Longer term things I can do to work towards this
goal over the next six months or so.

_____

_____

Things that I can do towards this goal in the next
month.

_____

_____

Things I can do towards this goal in the next
couple of weeks.

_____

_____

Goal 3: ....

Longer term things I can do to work towards this
goal over the next six months or so.

_____

_____

Things that I can do towards this goal in the next month.

_____

_____

Things I can do towards this goal in the next couple of weeks.

_____

_____

Try and make your goals specific to you. Make sure you can measure your progress with them, and that they are realistic for you to achieve.

Now you have your goals, rate each one for how much you are able to do it now, or how much progress you have made towards achieving it. This will be a baseline for you to look back on. By re-rating yourself as you continue through the book, it will allow you to measure how things are improving objectively.

Rating my goals

Goal 1: ....Today's date...................

I can do this now (circle a number):

0	1	2	3	4	5	6
Not at all		Occasionally		Often		Any time

One month re-rating (Today's date...................)
(circle a number):

0	1	2	3	4	5	6
Not at all		Occasionally		Often		Any time

Two month re-rating (Today's date...................)
(circle a number):

0	1	2	3	4	5	6
Not at all		Occasionally		Often		Any time

Three month re-rating (Today's date................)
(circle a number):

0	1	2	3	4	5	6
Not at all		Occasionally		Often		Any time

Goal 2:...............Today's date...................

I can do this now (circle a number):

0	1	2	3	4	5	6
Not at all		Occasionally		Often		Any time

One month re-rating (Today's date...................)
(circle a number):

0	1	2	3	4	5	6
Not at all		Occasionally		Often		Any time

Two month re-rating (Today's date...................)
(circle a number):

0	1	2	3	4	5	6
Not at all		Occasionally		Often		Any time

Three month re-rating (Today's date................)
(circle a number):

0	1	2	3	4	5	6
Not at all		Occasionally		Often		Any time

Goal 3:...............Today's date...................

I can do this now (circle a number):

0	1	2	3	4	5	6
Not at all		Occasionally		Often		Any time

One month re-rating (Today's date...................)
(circle a number):

0	1	2	3	4	5	6
Not at all		Occasionally		Often		Any time

Two month re-rating (Today's date...................)
(circle a number):

0	1	2	3	4	5	6
Not at all		Occasionally		Often		Any time

Three month re-rating (Today's date................)
(circle a number):

0	1	2	3	4	5	6
Not at all		Occasionally		Often		Any time

You have now thought about what life will be like if you make changes and set some goals. We hope that you feel motivated to continue. Keep going! In

Section 2, we are going to learn more about worry and GAD, share top tips from other people who have used the techniques in this book and consider how your own anxiety and worry is affecting you, what may be maintaining it and what can be done to help! Read on to find out more.

UNDERSTANDING GENERALISED ANXIETY DISORDER (GAD) AND THE ROLE OF WORRY

People who are experiencing Generalised Anxiety Disorder (GAD) have high levels of worry, often in the form of 'what if' thoughts about things that may happen in the future. Worrying can seem helpful at first to reduce the anxiety that the person experiences. Worrying too much, however, can interfere with their ability to do the everyday things they want to do in their life. People with GAD tell us that they find it difficult to control their worrying. The worries that people experience are usually about everyday events and things close to the person, such as family, health, finances, work or school. It is often the case that people with GAD worry about a range of things at any one time, although the focus of the worries can change over time according to what is going on in the person's life in that period. People with high levels of anxiety begin to worry about the fact they are worrying so much and what it means about them. For example, they may worry that their worrying is out of control and that they cannot stop their worrying thoughts.

Often people who worry a lot may also be concerned about the idea of not worrying, as they find that worry makes them feel that things are more certain, controllable or predictable in the short term. Having this level of worry can also impact upon the person's mood, with people often experiencing GAD along with a lowering in their mood.

People can feel trapped in a vicious circle of worry and anxiety. For example, they may have lots of physical tension or feel on edge. It may affect their sleeping or make them feel more irritable with other people around them. They may start to worry about their worrying itself and try not to worry as much, only for this to lead to further anxiety and worry and so on.

Although we all may worry at times, worry itself can become a problem when it doesn't lead to any helpful action, or is out of proportion to the situation and impacts upon the person's life. The diagram on page 26 shows the ways in which GAD can impact upon you physically, and can impact upon your thoughts and on what you do as a result. All of these areas have a knock-on effect on each other and can keep the problem going round and round, like a vicious circle. They keep you locked in a cycle of worry and anxiety.

GAD and worry impact upon all three of these areas and one thing leads to another. For example, worrying can lead to increased tension and irritability, which in turn can lead to avoiding situations that are anxiety-provoking, uncertain, unpredictable or hard to control. A person may also over-prepare for things, spending lots of time rehearsing or planning, or they may procrastinate and put things off. They may also seek reassurance from friends or family to reduce how anxious they are feeling. These changes in what they do as a result may give relief in the short term, but in the long term can lead to more problems such as a restricted life and increasing worry.

A very important thing about the diagram below is the way that these three things reinforce each other. It can become a vicious circle, a 'downward spiral' that maintains worry and anxiety and is hard to break out of. Furthermore, the negative effects can spill over into other areas of your life. So often you end up with secondary problems as a result. For example, the worry may make it difficult for you to attend or concentrate at work, or it may affect your relationship with others. It may also restrict your activities and impact upon your mood as a result. Tension, which is a physical symptom of worrying and generalised anxiety, can also lead to other physical problems, like headaches, an upset stomach and increased aches and pains.

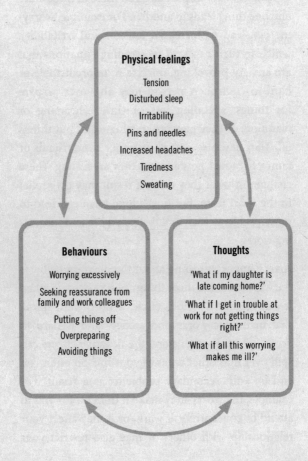

Physical feelings

Tension
Disturbed sleep
Irritability
Pins and needles
Increased headaches
Tiredness
Sweating

Behaviours

Worrying excessively
Seeking reassurance from family and work colleagues
Putting things off
Overpreparing
Avoiding things

Thoughts

'What if my daughter is late coming home?'
'What if I get in trouble at work for not getting things right?'
'What if all this worrying makes me ill?'

How is your own worry or GAD affecting you?

Each person may be affected differently in each of these areas and not all people have every symptom, but the ones in the diagram are commonly experienced ones. The good news is that there are ways of breaking into this vicious circle with the help of the techniques in this guide. There are techniques that will help you to target the main symptoms that you yourself are experiencing. Below is a blank vicious circle diagram so that you can complete your own symptoms. As in the example above, write into each of the three areas on the diagram below your own behaviours, thoughts and physical symptoms.

Meet Sarah and Graham

People who have used CBT self-help have said that reading case studies of other people who have experienced GAD is something they have found useful and encouraging. Two case studies are included in this self-help programme:

Graham is a 29-year-old office worker in a large company. He had been experiencing excessive worry, tension and anxiety about his work and health that was impacting upon his job and his relationship with his partner Emma.

Behaviours
(Things you have noticed
you are avoiding, or doing
more of as a result of how
your are feeling.)

_____
_____
_____
_____
_____

Thoughts
(Changes in your thinking.
Try to write them as the
specific thoughts that went
through your mind.)

_____
_____
_____
_____
_____

Physical
(Physical changes
you have noticed.)

_____
_____
_____
_____

Sarah was 44 and a married homemaker. She had always been a worrier, in fact her family used to joke about it when she was growing up. She experienced an episode of severe worry and anxiety when her husband Grant was made redundant and her twin daughters were both going away to university.

Whilst the personal situations of the people in these case studies may be different from your own, the techniques they have used are the same as the ones in this book that may help you. Throughout the programme we will return to the case studies to show you how they have put into action the techniques covered, and to highlight what went well and what may have been more challenging. Whilst the case studies highlight that using the CBT-based techniques to help to manage their GAD wasn't always easy, there were things that they did to overcome any challenges they faced and keep going.

It may not always be easy for you either, but being able to read through other people's experiences can help to keep you on track. Let's briefly meet Sarah and Graham who have shared their stories and find out more about their situations. If you want to read more at any time you can read their full stories and see their completed worksheets for how they used the techniques in Section 5.

Introducing Graham's Story

Graham was a 29-year-old salesman in a large company. He enjoyed his work and it was sociable as it was a large-team office environment. He met his partner Emma there a few years before. Graham had been promoted to the Team Leader for his section. Although he had always been prone to bouts of worry, taking on the extra responsibility at work had been particularly difficult for him. Since then, he had become more and more anxious and spent long periods of time worrying about whether he was doing a good enough job and if his manager was happy with the way he was managing the rest of his team. Graham also worried about his health and found he had more and more headaches than he had before, making him worry that there was something physically wrong with him; and about the flat he had bought and its maintenance. Graham and Emma were engaged and hoping to get married, but with his anxiety Graham found it really difficult to contemplate the wedding itself and he worried about the financial side of things.

His worries put a strain on his relationship with Emma as he was staying later and later in the office and taking work home with him in the evenings; something he never used to do before. Their social life was affected, as Graham would avoid certain situations in which he felt more anxious like travelling far from home, taking time off work or doing things he hadn't done previously. He had stopped drinking alcohol as he found it made him feel out of control, which was hard as most of their social group would go out for drinks in the evenings after work and for dinners at each other's houses. He was also asking Emma for reassurance by asking her to check his work after he had done it and getting her to take the responsibility for making the decisions about things in the home, their social life and finances as he struggled to make decisions and would put off dealing with things. A big symptom for Graham was tension, which compounded his headaches and led to him getting pain in his jaw and shoulders.

Graham successfully used the worry management technique and progressive muscle relaxation. This helped him to reduce his worrying and he got married to Emma the following summer in France!

You can find out how Graham got on with using the worry management technique and progressive muscle relaxation in Section 5 on page 121.

Introducing Sarah's story

Sarah was 44 and had been happily married to Grant since she was 27. They had twin daughters Emily and Olivia, who were 18 and had recently left home for the first time to go to university, four hours' drive away. Although Sarah was always a worrier, like her mother, things became very difficult for her when Grant was made redundant and Emily and Olivia moved so far away.

Sarah would spend long periods of time worrying during the day and the thought of not worrying made her feel even more anxious that something bad would happen. She particularly worried about Emily and Olivia going out at night and getting into trouble or danger as a result of them drinking. She would ring them every day and make them text her when they were going out and again when they got back to their student accommodation. As a result, Sarah worried even more until she got the text that they were back safely. She would try to plan ahead with them where they would be going and she would then look up the places online to see if they seemed safe.

Sarah also worried that because Grant had been made redundant that they would lose their home and not be able to pay off their mortgage and enjoy the retirement together they had planned in the future; even though Grant was actively looking for another job and had a good financial package from his company. Sarah would always plan things as far in advance as possible and liked to make lists and be in control of the family finances and other tasks. She worried that if Grant did any of those things they would go wrong. Despite Sarah wanting to take responsibility for these things, she often spent ages researching the best options, running everything past Grant for his opinion but then not actually getting round to completing the tasks, for example not paying off credit cards on time, leading to tension between her and Grant.

See how Sarah got on with using the worry management technique and problem solving in Section 5 on page 138.

Answering some questions you may have

Hopefully after reading the case studies you have begun to understand a little more about the ways in which different people may experience GAD and feel hopeful that the techniques they used may also help you to feel better too. You may still have a number of questions about the way in which GAD is affecting you and why you developed it in the first place. We will try to answer some of the common questions people with GAD often ask us so that hopefully any questions you have may be answered too.

Question 1: What is GAD?

GAD stands for Generalised Anxiety Disorder. People with GAD often find that they have a number of commonly experienced symptoms such as:

- Worry that is difficult to control

- Apprehensive expectation

- Tension

- Palpitations

- Sweating

- Dry mouth

- Problems concentrating

- Pins and needles

- Sleep difficulties

- Feeling on edge

- Putting things off (procrastinating)

- Avoiding things

- Over-preparing

- Seeking reassurance

The National Institute of Mental Health (NIMH) website has useful information about GAD. You can

read more on the website here: http://www.nimh.nih.
gov/health/topics/generalized-anxiety-disorder-
gad/ www.

Question 2: What causes GAD and why have I developed it?

There is no definite answer to what causes GAD to develop in some people but not others. What we do know, however, is that it involves social, biological and psychological vulnerabilities to anxiety. GAD does tend to run in families and the risk is higher if you have a close relative with it. It can also affect people who have had certain kinds of life events. So whilst research cannot at this stage categorically say what causes GAD for individuals, there are effective treatments that can help someone with it to manage it more effectively.

Question 3: What can be done about GAD?

The good news is that there are a number of things that can be done about GAD. There are evidence-based treatments, some of which are presented below. These are treatments that are recommended by the National Institute of Health and Care Excellence (NICE) as they have been researched extensively and are known to work for many people who use them.

CBT self-help (also known as Low Intensity CBT)

This is an example of the way you are working here. NICE recommends it as the first treatment for people with GAD, as a result of the good evidence base that exists supporting its use. The approach is based on Cognitive Behaviour Therapy, a psychological therapy that lends itself readily to a self-help format. CBT self-help consists of the same content and techniques that you would engage in if you were having face-to-face therapy with a trained therapist but is delivered in more flexible ways. The approach can be used without any support from a trained health professional, but having the support of someone to use the approach can be really effective. This is especially helpful if people really find themselves struggling with motivation or concentration to use it. The support provides encouragement and helps keep people on track if they are experiencing any difficulties. Many people use this type of approach with the support of their GP, nurse or (if in England) a Psychological Wellbeing Practitioner (PWP). If you think you would benefit from support to use this approach, you can ask your GP about what is available in your area or (if in England) you can find it here and self-refer: http://www.iapt.nhs.uk/services/ [www.]

Cognitive Behavioural Therapy (CBT)

In high-intensity CBT, people will attend regular sessions with a CBT therapist who will provide the treatment to help them overcome their GAD. However, there can be waiting lists due to the demand for treatment, and the availability of services varies tremendously by region. Also, if this way of working appeals to you, you should be careful to ask for CBT and should check that your therapist is accredited to deliver CBT with the British Association of Behavioural and Cognitive Psychotherapies (BABCP). This is your stamp of approval that the therapy actually has research to support its use and the practitioner is trained to deliver it.

Anti-anxiety medication

As well as there being CBT available to help you overcome your anxiety, there is also a range of different medications available. Some are more beneficial than others and so it is important to make an informed decision and know what you are being prescribed. Some people may feel that medication is the best way for them to help overcome their anxiety, some prefer to use CBT treatments such as this book and some prefer to use the two in combination. To some extent the best thing is to select what you feel is the best way for you. There is evidence for both medication and for psychological treatments like CBT.

Benzodiazepines

Traditionally, medications such as benzodiazepines were given for anxiety and they have been used since the 1960s. These medications are habit forming, create a tolerance and cause very unpleasant withdrawal symptoms. For that reason, those types of medications should only be prescribed for short-term use of two to four weeks, and they should not be stopped abruptly, but by using a reducing dose that has been calculated and agreed with your GP or psychiatrist. These types of medications can be unhelpful whilst you undertake a programme of CBT. This is because they reduce the anxiety you experience artificially and, as a result, your body does not learn that it does not need to produce it at these elevated levels. This can lead to needing more of the medication and its effectiveness decreasing, so you need to take more of it, and so on. The other problem with such medication is that it can be taken when you feel you need it and, as a result, people may carry it around with them when they go out – just in case they feel it's needed. If they then forget to bring it out, or don't have it with them, they feel panicky and anxious! These problems create a vicious circle that keeps anxiety going round.

Buspirone

Buspirone is a medication that is licensed for use for GAD. Like benzodiazepines it is only recommended for short-term use. It takes a while to build up to an effective level and similarly should not be stopped abruptly but with a planned decreasing dose from your GP. Buspirone works on serotonin levels in the brain. It can be helpful in short-term use, but isn't recommended for long periods of time.

Antidepressants

You may not be feeling depressed or low as well as anxious, but your GP or psychiatrist may have prescribed an antidepressant for your anxiety. Certain antidepressants from a family of medications called Selective Serotonin Reuptake Inhibitors (SSRIs) or Selective Noradrenalin Reuptake Inhibitors (SNRIs) can be prescribed for GAD. Usually a medication called Sertraline is prescribed first as this is recommended in guidelines for use with GAD; but other SSRIs can also be used. They can be used to treat anxiety for longer periods of time, so whilst you may not be feeling depressed it may be that your GP or psychiatrist has prescribed an antidepressant for its useful impact on anxiety. These medications do not reduce your anxiety straightaway. They build up over time to get to a therapeutic dose so it is important that you keep taking them and do not discontinue them without discussing this with your GP. Modern anti-depressants have fewer side effects and are not habit forming or addictive, as people often assume. They can cause discontinuation symptoms and, so again, stopping taking them is best done in partnership with your GP or psychiatrist. You can read more about antidepressants, dosages and side effects here:

http://www.nhs.uk/conditions/Antidepressant-drugs/Pages/Introduction.aspx www.

Question 4: I have digestive problems – is this connected?

We know that people with GAD have higher incidences of digestive disorders such as Irritable Bowel

Syndrome (IBS). When you are anxious and tense, this can affect your digestive system and many people with GAD also report symptoms of IBS such as constipation, diarrhoea, cramping and flatulence. Some people find that certain foods may trigger their symptoms. You can read more about IBS and things that may be helpful here: http://www.nhs.uk/Conditions/Irritable-bowel-syndrome/Pages/Symptoms.aspx www.

Question 5: Will treatment remove all my anxiety and worry?

Some anxiety is helpful; it keeps us safe and out of danger. Anxiety is a useful and functional emotion. If you stepped out to cross the road and a car was coming, having an anxiety-based adrenalin response helps you to jump back onto the pavement and out of harm's way. Having excessive anxiety and worry that is happening most of the time out of context with the situations you are facing is not helpful. Treatment aims to reduce the excessive anxiety and worry, but not to remove all anxiety completely; it will get it back into balance.

Question 6: Do I have to stop worrying altogether?

Often when people have worried for a long time, they have positive thoughts about their worrying, even though they find it difficult in other ways. Some people have concerns that if they stop worrying they will not manage things as effectively, or that aspects of their life might spiral out of control. These are more worries! People who worry a lot may think that worrying helps them to feel more certain in an unpredictable world. We all worry from time to time, so we are not aiming to remove all your worry, just the unproductive worry and anxiety that leads to no helpful action and that keeps you locked in that vicious circle.

The first step to tackling your worries is to capture them each time as they arise. Try and record your worries as actual thoughts that go through your mind. You can learn more about how to do this in Section 3. Before you turn the page, however, other people who have used these approaches to manage their GAD have given us some top tips to share with you; along with tips from practitioners like us who help people with GAD.

Top Tips!

1. 'I often worried at night, which would stop me dropping off to sleep, or I would wake up in the middle of the night worrying. Keeping a note pad and pen by the side of the bed to write the worries down, knowing I would come back to them at my scheduled Worry Time the next day, helped me to manage this. Eventually, I worried less and less at night and my sleep improved.'

2. 'When I first started trying to use the Worry Time technique, I found refocusing on what was going on around me really hard! It helped me to get up and go outside if I could or get up and have a walk into another room if I was at work.'

3. 'I thought I was really good at problem solving! It wasn't until I found out what problem solving actually should be that I learned that I was just good at worrying, but not so good at doing anything about the worries that I did need to take action about. I was a king of procrastinating!'

4. 'Through doing this I have learned the difference between helpful worrying that leads to me doing something about the problem and unhelpful worry which just leads me to feeling worse! That's probably the single most helpful thing that I have learned through this.'

5. 'It can be really hard to get going when you are feeling anxious, it can also be anxiety-provoking itself to think

about what life will be like when you don't worry as much anymore! I always tell the people I work with to think about all the spare time you will have for nice activities instead of worrying and how much more enjoyable they will be when you are in the moment focused on what you are doing, rather than being lost up in your head worrying.'

6. 'At first you can't imagine being able to worry for just a set time each day and the worries keep popping back up, but if you are consistent with the technique you learn that you can control your worries instead of them controlling you. Just keep trying it and see what happens.'

7. 'Tension is a really difficult symptom of GAD and one that can lead to more worry and anxiety, aches and pains and stress. If tension is a problem for you, practising progressive muscle relaxation is a fantastic way to help with this. It takes a while, so needs doing every day, but it really works and people find it really useful.'

Now you have learned more about GAD and the way it can affect people, created your own vicious circle diagram and heard top tips from others, it is time to get going with your own worry management plan! Turn the page to find out how ...

Section 3

MANAGING YOUR WORRY

Step 1: Recording and classifying your worries

To make managing your worries easier to tackle and personalised for you, we have broken down the techniques into steps. This is because different worries require different ways of managing them. You may use some or all of these steps depending on what type of worries you identify when completing Step 1 and also if you have identified that the physical symptom of tension is a problem for you when you identified your own symptoms in your vicious circle.

The first step to tackling your worries is to capture them each time as they arise and to classify them into the type of worry you have had (we explain more about this further on!). You don't have to take any other action to begin with. The reason that classifying the type of worry that you are having is important as a first step is because people have two types of worries and they need to be dealt with differently. This step sets our foundation for what to do next and gives us key information and data to help you to navigate through the interventions.

The two types of worries

The two types of distinct worries that we have are **practical worries** and **hypothetical worries**. When people experience high levels of worry in GAD, distinguishing between these two types becomes difficult. This can lead to not managing them as effectively as possible and keeping us locked in that vicious circle. One of the main differences between hypothetical and practical worries is the amount of control you have over the situation and what, if anything, can be done as a result. A difficulty arises if you try to deal with all your worries in the same way. When this happens your worries may soon start to feel overwhelming and you may get caught up in the vicious circle. This can then get in the way of you trying to take any action to sort any of your worries out and may cause you to start putting things off (procrastinating) or seeking reassurance from others.

Practical worries

Practical worries are about current practical problems. These are worries that are often about practical issues affecting you right now and for which there is a practical solution that could be taken. These types of worry usually happen less frequently, but need some action to be taken to solve them. Examples of such worries include finance or work matters. They tend to revolve around practical things, such as 'My credit card interest-free period runs out soon; what if I can't pay it off?' or 'What if I don't finish the tender document on time for submission?'

Hypothetical worries

Hypothetical worries are often about things that may be in the future and may not have a solution or action right now that we can take, no matter how hard we try to find one. For example: 'What if the plane crashes on the way to France next summer?' 'What if the bus to take me to the hospital is late tomorrow?' 'What if Dave falls out of love with me?' Or, 'What if I get a horrible illness when I am older?' Hypothetical worries may seem to be about practical things like relationships, flying or health, but there is no action that we can take right now about a flight next summer or even what may happen on the flight when that day arises.

When you are caught in a negative circle of worry it can be hard to differentiate between the two types of worry and take action on the ones you need to and let go of the ones you don't. Worrying all the time distracts you from what you are doing in the present and stops you from enjoying and being in touch with things in that moment. That can mean that you feel like you are not really part of what is going on around you and that you never get a break from worrying. People with GAD often say they feel lost up in their heads worrying rather than being focused on what they are doing. This means people spend long periods of time worrying over things that they do not need to worry about at that time and they don't take the action they need to take for more practical problems. Just starting to differentiate between these two types of worries at the time you are having them is helpful and starts to break that vicious circle. Initially it can be difficult to distinguish between them when we are anxious, especially when we are emotionally caught up in them and they are personal to us. To help with this, we have provided a worry classification tool that you can use to help you each time you record a worry. This is on page 60.

Key point

The key thing to remember about classifying your worries is that typically we worry about practical everyday things. So it can seem confusing as to which are practical, needing us to take action straightaway, and which are hypothetical. A useful way of remembering the difference is to consider whether there is any action you could or should take at the time you are having the worry. Although the worry might be about a practical issue in the future, if there is no action you could or should take towards dealing with it at the time you are having the worry, then it is hypothetical. For example, if you are in a meeting at work and need to concentrate on what your colleagues are saying, but you are worrying about managing a drive later in the week to an area you haven't been to before, then at the time you are having the worry it is hypothetical. It should be treated as a hypothetical worry as you cannot take any action in the meeting and you should be paying attention to the discussion taking place; so refocusing on that is important. Later on, when you are able, you can then take action to plan your trip (using the problem-solving technique if it is helpful to do this).

Why trying not to think about it doesn't work!

You may have tried strategies before to control your worries and not to think about them that have worked in the short term (or not!) but have not been effective in managing the problem in the longer term. One strategy many people attempt is to try not to think about a worry and think of something else. This is called thought suppression. When you tell yourself to stop worrying, or try and think of something else, it is only distracting you from the worry in the short term. This can actually lead to a rebound effect where you end up with more worrying thoughts, which then gain more power. Thought suppression can be maintained for a little while, but requires such focus it is exhausting to do and leaves little space for you to do anything else. You can test this out for yourself if you want to, using the penguin experiment below!

Penguin experiment

For this experiment you need nothing other than 10 minutes of your time and a stopwatch or timer. There are two parts to the experiment. You can either do both parts yourself or if you have a friend or loved one with you, you could ask them to do one of the parts at the same time as you do the other and compare notes at the end.

Part 1:

For five minutes you can think about anything you want to, including thinking about a black and white penguin. Just spend five minutes sitting and noticing what comes into your mind. Any thought is OK and you can stay with that thought as long as you want to; don't try to push any thought away. When you have a thought of a penguin, just note it on a tally chart.

Part 2:

For five minutes you must try NOT to think about a black and white penguin. You can do anything you want to stop yourself thinking about a black and white penguin. Each time the thought or image of a penguin comes back into your mind, make a tally chart of it.

When you have finished both parts (or if you are working with a friend or loved one when you have both finished) compare the tally charts. What do you notice? Most people find that when they try not to think about something, it actually happens more! Pushing the thought away and trying to supress it, like in Part 2 of the experiment, leads to more of the thoughts that they do not want. What did you do to not think about it? People trying to avoid thinking about certain things often end up thinking about similar themes instead; for example, in this instance a pink penguin or another creature from a cold climate! What does this teach us about thought suppression? What does this mean for trying to supress worries? Research has shown that it leads to more worries, more anxiety and similar worrying thoughts along the same theme, as well as taking lots of time and effort! So trying not to think about your worry leads to more worry, more anxiety and more thoughts around the same topic of your worry. So it is definitely more helpful to use the strategies you can learn in this book, which are more effective ways of managing worry!

When and how to write worries down

For at least three days (up to a week) keep a record of your worries as and when they occur so that we can distinguish the type of worries that you are having and their impact. This means that we can then decide on the best intervention to help with them. We have provided you with a Worry Diary to use in the section below. There are also blank copies of this diary on page 172.

Each time you notice a worry in your mind, write down the date and time, what situation you are in, what the worry is that you have had and how anxious it made you feel on a 0–10 scale where 0 is not at all anxious and 10 is the most anxious you could possibly be (e.g. panic). By recording your worries for a few days, you can see in what situations they tend to occur, when they tend to happen, how much you actually worry and notice the different types of worries that you have. This will help you to ensure that the intervention that you use next is going to be the most useful one for you.

When you write down your worries, try and record them as the actual thoughts that go through your mind. For example, 'What if I get stuck in traffic and I miss the meeting?' or 'Will my daughter come home safely from school?' Write them down as soon as you can after the thought has gone through your mind. Try not to leave a big gap between it happening and recording it. Some people have even recorded them into their phone or electronic device if they cannot write something down at the time, and then copied these onto the diary at a later stage. Whatever way of recording them that suits you is fine as long as you record and classify them! (Be sure to have a pen and the worksheet, or something you can record into with you in your pocket or bag.)

At a good time for you, it is important to transfer all your worries onto the Worry Diary if you have not recorded them directly onto it. Once you have kept your Worry Diary for a few days, then you can complete the reflective questions on page 60.

If you worry at night

Many people find they worry more at night and this gets in the way of them falling or staying asleep. If this is the case for you, keep whatever you are using to record your worries and a pen next to the side of your bed. Then if you find yourself worrying at night write down the worry, turn back off the light and try to get to sleep knowing you will come back to it later.

If the same worry keeps coming back

Sometimes the same worry can keep popping back into your mind when you are completing your Worry Diary. If that is the case for you, just write it down again and classify it. It does not matter how many times you write the same worry down. If it is a hypothetical worry just write it down again and re-focus on the present. Don't be surprised if the worry bounces back a few times; that is normal. Over time, this will reduce. Notice and record if the situation or emotional reaction you get is different and record these as they occur. It may be worth checking that you are happy that you have classified the worry correctly; if you have, and it is a hypothetical one (one where there is nothing that can be done and no action that you could or should take at the time you are having the worry), that's fine. These are the exact ones we want to write down. Worries can keep popping back into your mind. We will use a strategy to help manage these types of worries later in this section. If the worry that keeps coming back is practical (and at the time you are having it there is an action you should take to manage it), then the problem-solving technique in this book will help you to manage it and you should follow the steps to deal with it using that.

To begin with you may find it helpful to have the classifying tool with you to help you decide what type of worry it is. Over time as you become used to classifying worries you may find that you can do it in your mind when you are having the worry. This will be great and something to work towards, as it is a way of managing your worries more productively and being able to do this will help you to improve how you are feeling. To begin with, because all this may be very new, write your worries down in the Worry Diary and then use the 'Classifying Your Worries' decision tree each time.

Worry Diary Table

Date & Time	Situation (where you are, what you are doing and what is going on around you)	Your Worry (e.g. 'What if......')	How anxious do you feel on a 0–10 scale? (0–not at all anxious, 10–the most anxious you have ever been)	Practical (P) or Hypothetical (H)? (tick the column below)	
				P	H

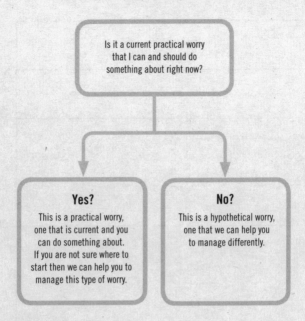

Is it a current practical worry that I can and should do something about right now?

Yes?

This is a practical worry, one that is current and you can do something about. If you are not sure where to start then we can help you to manage this type of worry.

No?

This is a hypothetical worry, one that we can help you to manage differently.

Reflecting on your Worry Diary

Once you have completed your Worry Diary for a few days (a minimum of three days and up to a week), completing these reflective questions will help you to see which techniques may be most helpful for you to use first. Take out your diary sheet(s) and look at the worries that you have had over the time you have been completing it:

1. What do you notice when you look at the worries that you have been having?

2. What type of worry have you had more of, practical or hypothetical?

3. Did you have difficulty in classifying any of your thoughts?

4. When you had a practical worry about a problem, did you take action on it to deal with it at the time, when you realised it was a practical worry?

5. If you notice that you had more hypothetical worries, how often during the day do you have them?

6. Are all your hypothetical worries still relevant and a problem by the end of the day, or by the following day?

7. What does that tell you about hypothetical worries?

Once you have reflected upon your Worry Diary, it is time for you to make a decision about which intervention you feel is the one that would be most helpful for you to use first. We have provided a short summary of the interventions in the box below and what they are used for. If you haven't already done so, you can read more about the interventions in the stories of Graham and Sarah in Section 5 on page 121. This will enable you to decide which of these you wish to use.

THE INTERVENTIONS

The Worry Time technique for hypothetical worries

For many people with GAD they find that they have more hypothetical than practical worries. These worries take up much of their day (and often can affect their sleeping too). The good news is that there is something that can be done about these types of worries. There is a technique that you can use that can help you to manage them more effectively, called Worry Time. Many, many people have used the Worry Time technique to help them to manage their hypothetical worries. In Worry Time, you allow yourself to worry as much as you want, but only at the time that you choose to. It helps you to gain control over your worries instead of them controlling you. It takes time and practice and at first you may think that you couldn't possibly manage not to worry outside of your Worry Time. We will help you with that, using a technique that helps to refocus your mind away from your worries outside of your planned Worry Time.

Practical problem solving for current practical problems

Some people with GAD find that when a current practical problem arises which they should take action on, they are so caught up in their worry and anxiety that they struggle to take the action they need to take. It can also affect the way in which they respond to the problem, with the anxiety it causes putting them off from dealing with it. They may also have sought reassurance from other people to help them to deal with things, or want other people rather than themselves to take the responsibility for making decisions for them or taking action when something needs doing. This can then undermine their confidence when they need to tackle something by themselves. Problem solving is a skill and, as with any skill, practising it helps us to embed the skill so that we can do it more easily in the future. It can help us to think things through and consider options, make decisions and take the best course of action for us. We can all benefit from using problem solving, and people with GAD who have a practical worry they have not taken any action about, or that don't know how to start dealing with, find it really effective.

Progressive Muscle Relaxation (PGMR)

Progressive Muscle Relaxation (PGMR) is a technique that helps you to manage tension if this is a particular physical symptom that you experience, or if you have noticed that you have headaches, aches and pains or other problems that can be caused by holding your body tense as a result of your worrying. When we worry about things and feel anxious, the body's muscles can tense. Muscular tension can lead to stiffness, pain and discomfort and also affect your posture and joint stability. Because the worry is usually about something in the future – e.g. 'What if I am late for work this morning?' – our body goes into a freeze response (one of the adrenalin responses we have to either fight, flight, freeze or flop in response to something threatening that makes us anxious or fearful). We tense up our muscles and hold on to that tension. We can carry it around with us long after the anxiety or worry has passed, leaving us feeling achy or stiff. Our muscles do not learn the difference between feeling tense or relaxed and so we can carry ourselves around tensed up during the day even when we are not worrying, further compounding the problem. PGMR helps your muscles to learn the difference between being relaxed and tensed up, so that they can spot when you are tensing up and let it go. PGMR, like any skill, requires practice but is a really effective strategy for managing tension as well as preventing physical pain and discomfort.

Where to go next

Now you have read a little about the three techniques, you may feel that one or more of these would be beneficial for you to use for the particular symptoms and type of worries that you noted in your Worry Diary. If you want to use the Worry Time technique, then this is Step 2, which starts below. If you want to use the problem-solving technique, this is Step 3 on page 77, and if you wish to begin to use PGMR each day, then this is in Step 4 on page 88. You do not have to do these steps in order, some people find they do not need to use a particular technique, so choose the ones that are most relevant to you. You can use PGMR at the same time as the other steps, as this is a technique that you would practise every day.

Step 2: The Worry Time technique

If you have noticed that you have a large number of hypothetical worries, you are not alone. Most people with GAD report high levels of hypothetical worries. Having lots of these worries does not mean that they are not about something that is real or important to you. It is the timing of when they are popping into your mind and the number of them that you have that isn't helpful. As we have mentioned, when you are worrying it distracts your focus away from what you are doing in the present moment onto future concerns. This can keep you in that vicious circle of worry and prevents you from feeling fully able to enjoy what you are doing in that moment.

Worry Time is a strategy for managing hypothetical worries more effectively. In Worry Time you allow yourself to worry; in fact, you can worry as much as you like, for as long as you like, but only during a set time that you choose and are in control of. Outside of Worry Time, you refocus on the present moment and learn a way to let go of the worry, safe in the knowledge that you can come back to it and worry about it as much as you want in your Worry Time. Sometimes it can be hard just to let go of those hypothetical worries, even if they don't have a current or practical solution. If you did the penguin experiment earlier in this section, you will have learned that thought suppression (trying not to think about your worry) isn't helpful and only distracts you temporarily and may actually have the opposite effect of giving you more worries! We need a more effective way of managing them! Worry Time allows you to worry about things, but at a time that you are in control of, and in a tried and tested way. It is the exact opposite of thought suppression and distraction; those techniques we know do not work in the longer term and keep you locked in that vicious circle.

Initially, many people think there is no way that they will manage with just one period a day they can worry in, and believe they have so many worries that there is no way this could work, but it really does help. It takes time and practice, but it is a really effective tool that you are in control of using. Imagine what life will be like if you can free up the rest of your day to not worry and to be more focused and engaged in what is going on around you – give it a try for a couple of weeks and see; what have you got to lose! If you want to read about someone else's experience of using Worry Time, turn to page 121 and read the recovery stories of Graham and Sarah if you haven't already done so. They both used Worry Time, and initially had exactly the same worries about giving up their worrying and whether the time they set aside to worry each day would be enough! But it really helped them and can really help you too.

To help you to use Worry Time we have broken it down into stages for you to follow.

Stage 1: Plan your Worry Time

Plan a time that you can always use as your Worry Time. This will be a set time for you to worry in. Consider how long you feel you need, and how long is an acceptable period for you to set aside each day, fitted around any other commitments that you have. How long you initially choose to have for your Worry Time is entirely up to you; you can review this after the first few times and see how long you need. For example, you may choose a worry period at 7 p.m. and decide that you will worry for 30 minutes, or even an hour. The time should be your decision. Whatever time of the day works for you is fine; however, this should be a time you set aside just for you to worry and you should not do anything else during this time but worry. Ensure that any potential distractions are reduced. For example, make sure that others are aware that they should not bother you during this time, direct your phone to answerphone, and so forth. Don't do it when you are at work or when your favourite TV programme that you want to watch is on!

Write your Worry Time plan in the box below:

My planned Worry Time is .... AM/PM
and I will worry for .... minutes

Stage 2: Write down your hypothetical worries throughout the day

Each day start with a fresh **My Hypothetical Worries Today** sheet. When you notice you are worrying outside of your planned Worry Time and it is a hypothetical worry, write it down on the sheet. At first, you may find it useful to use the classifying tool from Step 1 to do this if you are not sure if the worry is hypothetical or practical.

If it is a current practical worry that you can do something about, and there is an action that you should and can take at that time, you should take the action to solve the problem. Practical worries do not need to be written on this sheet. If it is a hypothetical worry, write it down knowing that you can worry about it as much as you like in your planned Worry Time later that day.

Each time you have a hypothetical worry and have written it down, use Stage 3 to refocus on the present and complete the Worry List, stating what activity you are going to do to refocus.

If you get more hypothetical worries during the day, just repeat the process throughout the day, writing them down and refocusing on the present using an activity you have written down. You may find the same hypothetical worries keep coming back. That is OK too, just write them down again and focus on the present, knowing what activity you are going to do to refocus and also that you can worry as much as you want about them during your Worry Time later in the day.

If you find you worry a lot at night when you are trying to get off to sleep, or wake up during the night worrying, you may find it useful to keep a new Worry List at the side of the bed with a pen so that you can write each one down and then refocus on the task at hand – sleeping. Use Stage 3 to refocus your attention on the present. Notice where you are and what is going on around you. Notice the feel of the duvet against your skin, etc. Get comfortable and try to go back to sleep, knowing that you can worry about it as much as you want during your next Worry Time. You can repeat this as often as you need to.

Stage 3: Refocus on the present moment you are in

Once you have written down a worry on your Worry List, the next stage of the Worry Time technique is to refocus on the present moment. This means paying attention to what you were doing before you were worrying, or what is going on around you and the task at hand. You may find it helpful to start a new activity and really pay attention to it, using your senses. For example, imagine you were sat on the sofa with the TV on and noticed you were worrying about a hypothetical worry instead of watching the TV programme fully; you would write the worry on your Worry List, then refocus on the task at hand – watching TV. You could turn up the volume or change channel and really pay attention to the present moment and the conversation the people on TV are having.

Refocusing on the present moment means genuinely focusing your attention on a task, a conversation, a sound, the touch of things around you or your other senses at that moment. You may find it helpful to get up and change room, go outside for a few moments and notice what is going on around you and what you can hear or see. You could start a new task or do something different than you were doing before your started worrying. Whatever helps you to refocus on what is going on around you in the present moment is fine. Remember, the worry is distracting you from the present moment; your task is to beat it at its own game, by actively paying focused attention to what is happening around you and what you are doing in the moment. Don't let the worry distract you from what you are doing in the present. Even if you are for example sat at your desk at work and can't start something new or get up and move around, pay attention to the sounds around you in your office, for example, or the feel of your chair, or maybe stretch your arms and legs, make a phone call, read something on your screen or desk, or start a conversation with someone nearby.

Stage 4: Now worry in your scheduled Worry Time!

Each day, when your Worry Time comes around, you are going to allow yourself to worry about the things on your list during the time you have set aside. Go through the list of worries you have recorded since your last Worry Time and choose one that you would like to start to worry about. Then worry about it! You can worry as much as you want about it. Then, when you feel ready to, move to the next and so on. You have as much time as you have set aside for your Worry Time to spend worrying about the things you have written down. If some of the worries that you wrote down are no longer a problem for you when it comes to your Worry Time, then put a line through them and let them go.

At the end of your Worry Time you need to refocus on the present and stop worrying about the things on your old Worry List; they now belong to your last Worry Time and you will start a new Worry List for your next Worry Time. To help to do this some people like to throw away their Worry List after their Worry Time, or screw up the papers and put them into the bin afterwards to help them let go! Always start with a new list and fresh paper each day so that you only focus on the worries that have happened since your last Worry Time. Worry Time takes practice and repetition, but is a really useful and effective technique to help you manage your worry.

At the end of your Worry Time, spend some time reflecting on what you have noticed:

- Consider how you felt when you wrote the worries down and how you feel about them now.

- Has the thing you were worrying about happened?

- How did you deal with it if it did?

- Were there any worries that were no longer a problem when you came back to them during your Worry Time?

- Also reflect on what it feels like to worry as much as you want for that period of time. Could you keep worrying or did your mind wander, for example?

- When you have used Worry Time for a few days, consider if you need as much time as you planned in Stage 1? If not, you can always reduce it down. As you go forwards with Worry Time each day you will hopefully find that you feel less worried outside of your Worry Time and that you feel more able to manage your worries more effectively.

Remember: Refocus on the present moment

It is refocusing on the present that helps you to manage your worries outside of your scheduled Worry Time. At the end of your Worry Time remember to refocus on the present moment and away from your worries, even if some of them still feel current. To refocus on the present you may find it helpful to notice what you are doing or what is going on around you at that moment and tune your attention into it. Use your senses and be aware of what you can notice in that present moment, as that can help you. Getting up and doing something different or moving rooms from the one you have spent your Worry Time in may help. If your worries come back into your mind after your Worry Time that's OK; just write them down on your new day's worry sheet to worry about again at your next scheduled Worry Time and refocus on the present again by focusing your attention using the strategies we have described.

My hypothetical worries today

My Hypothetical Worries Today	
My scheduled Worry Time is:_____am/pm for:_____mins	
My Worry:	To refocus on the present moment I am now going to:
e.g. What if I have made a mistake at work?	e.g. Put the radio on and cook dinner (spaghetti) and notice the lovely smells and sing along!

How long should you continue with the Worry Time technique?

As with all new skills, learning to take control of your worry during your day, rather than letting it control you, will take time. There is no definite amount of time it will take for the technique to work. It is about practice. At times it may be hard to manage your worry and refocus; at other times, practical problems may get mixed into your Worry List and you may realise you have a worry that is actually a practical current problem that you can solve and take action on. The key thing is that each day, through practising the Worry Time technique, you are breaking the vicious circle of worry and anxiety. It may take a few weeks, or longer for you to begin to feel less anxious and feel more in control of your worries; just like it took time for the vicious circle to build and take hold, it will take time to undo it as well. Things won't happen overnight, but slowly and surely the technique has worked for many people. You can keep going with the technique for as long as you want to. We recommend that when you get to the point of thinking you no longer need it, keep going just a little bit longer and then move on to Step 4 – relapse prevention. Remember, now you have learned how to use the Worry Time technique it is always there should you need it again in the future.

Step 3: Practical problem solving

Practical problem solving is an effective technique that has seven short stages for managing practical worries. When we worry a lot, our problems can sometimes feel overwhelming, as though there are no solutions. Problem solving is an evidence-based technique that helps you to step back from your current practical worry to help you to choose which of the different practical solutions to the problem is best for you to take.

A 'current practical worry' is one that you need to take action on straightaway and that is a practical problem external to you, like choosing which credit card to switch to, or organising quotes for work on your house for repairs that need fixing. If you have been struggling to know where to start in dealing with a practical problem, have been putting off dealing with it or feel overwhelmed by the problem, then practical problem solving is for you. We have broken the technique into stages to help you to work through it. You can use it for any current practical worry that arises. Problem solving is a skill; using it and practising using the stages will help you to feel more confident in solving practical problems as they arise in the future.

Stage 1: Write down your practical worry and convert it into a problem to be solved

If you identify a current practical worry that you would like to try and problem solve, the first stage is to write this in the space in **Worksheet A** on page 84 and to convert the worry into the specific practical problem you need to solve and when it needs to be solved by. Worries are often phrased like questions, or are not as clear or specific as they need to be in order for us to solve them, which can be overwhelming and stop us from taking the action we need to solve the problem. For example, if your worry is 'I haven't paid my council tax' then convert this into a specific practical problem and when it needs to be done by, such as 'I need to pay the council tax by Friday this week by ensuring I can get to the council tax office to pay during my lunchbreak or arrange time out of work to do it when the council office is open'.

Stage 2: Think of as many solutions as possible

You should then try to identify as many potential solutions as possible to the practical problem. At this stage nothing should be ruled out, no matter how ridiculous or impossible some solutions may seem. In fact, the ridiculous ones can help to get your ideas flowing to generate other more practical solutions. Write each solution onto **Worksheet A.**

Stage 3: Consider the strengths and weaknesses of each of the solutions you have identified

Next to each potential solution, write down any strengths or weaknesses of that solution for you and your present circumstances on **Worksheet A.** You may have generated an excellent solution, but it may not be possible to apply it in the time or within the resources you have available, for example. Consider how possible it is within the time you have to solve the problem, the resources you have available to you and how you feel about doing it. Doing this helps you to work out which solution you would like to choose and try first in Stage 4.

Stage 4: Rank your solutions and choose the one you want to try to carry out first

The next stage on **Worksheet A** is to rank the potential solutions in number order of how likely it would be that you would choose them, with number 1 being the solution that you think would be the most likely one you would want to try and carry out and the highest being the least likely or effective option. This should be based on the strengths and weaknesses of the solution that you listed in Stage 3. Ranking them in number order means that should the first solution that you choose to try out not fully solve the problem for you, or not be as effective as you had hoped, you can go back and carry out your second ranked option for example. Sometimes you never know which is the best solution to carry out to solve a particular problem until you put it into action and try it.

Stage 5: Make a plan to carry out your number 1 solution

Once you have chosen your solution, break it down into stages to consider what you need to do to carry it out. For example, if it involves calling a company, you need to have their number with you to call them. You may need to have an account number or a pen and paper handy. Thinking through the steps needed to carry out the solution helps you to plan for things that may happen so you feel confident in dealing with them. When you are making your plan on **Worksheet B** (page 86), complete the important W questions: **What** are you going to do? **When** are you going to do it? **Where** are you going to do it? And do you need anyone **With** you to be able to carry out your plan? Try and visualise carrying it out as you do it. This will help you to think through your plan. The W questions really help you to make your plan achievable and realistic. The more you think through the answer to the questions, the more likely it is that you will feel able to carry out your solution. If your plan involves carrying out the action on a different day and time to now, then make sure you make a note of it in your diary; you can also set yourself a reminder on your tablet or smartphone, or leave a note somewhere visible that you will see to remind you!

Stage 6: Carry out your chosen solution

Once you have a clear plan and have decided what you are going to do, where you are going to do it and when you are going to carry it out – then do it at your set time!

Don't be tempted to skip ahead to this stage without using Stages 2–5. These are really vital stages in managing practical worry. Although it might seem tempting just to think of a solution and get on with it, which is what you may have done before, it won't be as effective in helping you manage your practical worries in the longer term. The stages of problem solving are a process and, just like any process, missing parts of it can mean it doesn't have the desired effect.

Stage 7: Review the outcome!

When you have completed your chosen solution it is time to review the outcome using **Worksheet B**. Reflect on how the solution that you tried went. Did the solution you chose solve the problem? Was it partially solved, leaving something still to do; or did it completely solve it?

The advantage of problem solving is that other options often always exist. If you did not solve the problem using your first chosen solution, you have your other solutions ranked on **Worksheet A** that you can go back to. We can't always solve things first time, and often, until we put a solution into practice, we don't know how well it will work for us. The key thing is to get back into action and use the next solution (number 2 if number 1 hasn't worked, and so on).

If it did solve the problem, then that's great! You have broken the vicious circle and, any time that you need to, just by repeating these seven stages, you can continue to keep it in reverse by using practical problem solving for other current practical problems that may arise for you. Reflect on how it felt to complete the task and how the solution worked for you. What does this tell you about your ability to solve future or current problems?

How long should you continue to use practical problem solving?

Like any skill, practical problem solving requires practice. You can use the steps of problem solving any time you have a current practical problem that requires you to take action on it. You can continue to use it for as long as you want to and you always have the steps and skills to use it again in the future should you ever need to. There is no right and wrong to how many times or how often you should use the technique. As it is based on solving a current practical problem that arises in your daily life, it all depends on what current practical worries arise for you. It isn't something that needs practising every day like Worry Time or progressive muscle relaxation (PGMR) as it is a technique that you use as and when you need it for the practical and current worries that you have. Practical problem solving is really effective for helping you to break down and deal with current practical things happening in your life.

For those hypothetical worries, don't forget you can use the Worry Time technique. You can use each technique for the different type of worries that you have. You may also want to use progressive muscle relaxation (PGMR) if you experience tension, aches, pains, headaches or other physical symptoms of worrying and GAD. You can learn more about PGMR and how to practise it next!

Worksheet A

My current practical problem is:

Proposed Solutions	Strengths	Weaknesses	Ranking

Worksheet B

Putting the solution into action:	Reviewing the outcome:
What are you going to do?	How did it go?
When are you going to do it?	Has it solved the problem sufficiently?
Where are you going to do it?	If not go back to your list of ranked solutions on **Worksheet A** and put the next one into action, planning – on a new **Worksheet B** – what you are going to do and when you are going to do it.

Is there anyone you need with you?

Are there any things you need to do first?

Is there anything that might get in the way of your plan?
What can you do to overcome these obstacles?

If it went to plan and solved the problem, great! What have you learned from doing it that you can apply to the next practical problem that you have?

Step 4: Progressive Muscle Relaxation (PGMR)

Progressive muscle relaxation (PGMR) is a really useful technique that has been used for over fifty years for managing the tension and associated physical symptoms that occur in people with GAD. Our bodies have a resting level of muscle tension. Some people carry around more tension at rest, particularly if they are anxious or stressed. That tension can cause a range of physical aches and pains, stiffness and tightness in the muscles. This is often experienced in the neck, shoulders, jaw, stomach or other places in the body. When the body carries itself around with tension in the muscles, it can cause us to feel fatigued or more irritable. It can give us headaches, more pain, digestive problems and upset and can affect our sleep. The tension itself can make you feel more anxious, keeping you in that vicious circle.

When you are anxious in GAD and worrying, your body produces an adrenalin response (known as fight, flight, freeze or flop). In GAD the body prepares for action, but the threat (the content of the worry) is not located in the present moment and so our body goes into a freeze response when there isn't a present threat to deal with. We often hold on to this tension. PGMR aims to release it.

PGMR is a technique that was developed to help your body recognise when muscles are in a tense state and return them to a relaxed one. With regular practice, PGMR has been shown to reduce the muscle tension that you carry around and therefore improve the physical symptoms experienced as a result of anxiety and tension.

When you are anxious, have you noticed that you tense up, hold yourself tight or curl up your shoulders? This is a natural response in the face of the perceived threat (the worry), but because the worry that we have is out of proportion to the situation we are in, the result is lots of tension. Tension can act as a trigger for more worrying and keep the vicious circle going.

So, if you feel that PGMR would be helpful for you, you can follow these easy stages. PGMR should be practised once or (if you can, initially) twice daily, at a regular time that suits you. The more practice you do, the better your body will learn the difference between a tense and relaxed state and the easier it will be for you to release any tension you notice you are holding on to or you experience when you are anxious. You should set about 15 to 30 minutes aside for your practice each time. You may want to wear comfortable clothing and choose a regular time each day when you will not be disturbed. Keep the practice going to get the most benefits. This technique can really help to reduce your tension and assist your body to respond more helpfully in the future by learning the difference between holding your muscles tense or relaxed.

Key point: PGMR should be practised at a regular set time each day, once or twice only. Don't begin to practise it when you are feeling anxious. It is designed to help your muscles return to a relaxed state and learn to carry less tension around, and needs regular practising to be beneficial.

If you have a physical health condition, back pain or injury: Before practising PGMR, consult with your GP if you have a physical health condition, a current or previous serious injury, experience muscle spasms, or have back/joint problems. The deliberate muscle tensing of the PGMR procedure could exacerbate any of these pre-existing conditions. If you use PGMR without checking with your GP you do so at your own risk. If your GP says you are good to go, then follow the PGMR stages below.

Stage 1: Getting ready

Sit comfortably in a chair, you should sit to complete this technique and be awake. You can close your eyes if you want to, but equally they are fine open. You should remove any footwear.

Stage 2: Applying tension to different muscle groups one by one (five seconds of tension)

As you begin your 15 to 30 minutes of PGMR, you are going to tense isolated muscle groups in parts of your body and then release them in Stage 3. You can work from the top of your body to your feet, or from your feet upwards – it is entirely up to you. The key thing is that you focus on one muscle group at a time. Only hold the tension for five seconds, as this may feel uncomfortable initially or could lead to cramping if you hold it for too long. As you are tensing the muscle group it is important to notice and pay attention to what the muscle group feels like when it is tense, and then move to Stage 3. We have provided a list of muscle groups for you to work through below. You may find it helpful to have this list with you when you practise your PGMR.

Stage 3: Releasing the tension in the muscle group (15 seconds)

When you have held the muscle group you are working on tense for five seconds and noticed what it feels like to be tense, then it is time to relax that muscle group. Focus on what it feels like to release the tension and notice how the muscle group feels in a relaxed state. Recognising the difference in how the muscle group feels tense or relaxed is a key part of PGMR and of helping your body to learn to let go of tension in the future. Spend 15 seconds with the muscle group in that relaxed state, and then you can move to the next muscle group, repeating Stages 2 and 3 for each muscle group.

Which muscle groups should I tense?

When you practise PGMR each time, you should work either up or down the body to tense and release the tension in different muscle groups. For example:

- Your forehead: lift your eyebrows as high as you can and hold them tense.

- Your face: tighten up the muscles in your face and hold them tense.

- Your jaw: hold your jaw slightly open and tense.

- Your neck and shoulders: lift up your shoulders to your neck and hold the tension.

- Your right arm at the top: tighten your bicep muscle and tense it as if showing someone your muscles.

- Your left arm at the top: repeat as above with your left bicep.

- Your right hand and forearm: make a fist and tense your lower arm and stretch it out, keeping it tense.

- Your left hand and forearm: repeat the above with your left side.

- Your upper back and shoulder blades: stretch up your back and shoulder blades and hold them tense.

- Your abdomen and lower back: pull in your tummy muscles and hold them tight and tense.

- Your buttocks: tighten your buttocks and tense them up.

- Your entire right leg: put your leg out and tense it all the way down.

- Your entire left leg: repeat the above on your left side.

- Your lower right leg and calf: tense your calf muscle in your lower leg.

- Your lower left leg and calf: repeat the above with your left side.

- Your right foot: curl up your toes and tense your foot.

- Your left foot: repeat the above with your left foot.

After your PGMR practice

After you have tensed and relaxed each muscle group, you may find some muscle groups still feel tense. You can repeat the practice on that muscle group to leave it in a relaxed state. When you have released the tension in each muscle group, stay with the relaxed muscle feeling in your entire body for a few minutes and think about what it feels like to have released the tension in your body and what you notice; then you can get up from the chair and end your practice.

How long should I carry on with PGMR?

PGMR should be practised daily and may be something you wish to carry on with in the longer term.

Hopefully, through regular practice the amount of tension you hold becomes less and less and you notice your body releases tension for you automatically. You may also notice if you are tense and be able to let the muscle group relax, because you have noticed the difference and how it feels in your body. You should practise for at least a month, once or twice daily for best results, but many people carry on with PGMR or use a shortened version as daily practice.

At first, you may feel achy, as you are tensing muscles and maybe using muscle groups that you do not use that often. A little discomfort in the tension stage is to be expected. However if you find that the pain is significant you should stop and check this out with your GP.

MANAGING THE FUTURE

Now you have completed the techniques to manage your worry and are hopefully feeling less anxious and more able to manage your worries, it is time to think about the future (in a non-hypothetical way!). It is also time to congratulate yourself and for big congratulations from us.

You have committed time and hard work in putting the techniques into action in your daily life. You have successfully helped yourself to feel better, broken the vicious circle of worry and anxiety, and learned techniques that you can use any time you want to, both now and in the future. You made the change and you have the tools to keep your progress going.

Re-rating your goals

At this point it is also helpful to go back to the goals that you set for yourself at the start of the book and to see how you have progressed towards them and whether there is any further work to reach them that you would still like to do. Turn to page 19 to re-rate them and then join us back here when you have done it.

If after rating your goals there are still some things that you would like to do, you can! Make a plan and use the techniques you have learned until you feel that you have completed them. If you have reached your goals, that is great! You are ready to take the next and final step. This step is designed to help you to keep up the progress you have made, to think about continuing to manage your worries more effectively, and to feel confident to deal with any difficulties that you may face in the future. We really encourage you to complete this last step and work through this section.

Reaching this point is a really positive sign that things have improved. But also it can understand-ably be a time when you are concerned about your anxiety coming back, and losing the progress you have made.

Sometimes people at this stage may have concerns such as:

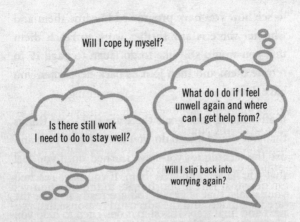

If a practitioner has been supporting you to work through this book, being discharged can also be concerning. You may wonder if you are ready or able to face going it alone without that support. Remember, it isn't the support from the practitioner alone that has helped you to feel better. It is the work you have done between sessions in your daily life using Worry Time, practical problem solving and progressive muscle relaxation that have achieved that. You have learned skills that will enable you to help yourself again should you ever need to. Now you are feeling better, you know you can do so, if necessary.

When someone has experienced GAD and now feels better, it is understandable that they don't want to feel highly anxious again. For some people, however, this in itself can become a source of concern and worry. They then try to avoid getting unwell again at all costs, which frequently means that they look out for any signs or symptoms of feeling unwell. They may mistake normal mood fluctuations of feeling anxious or worrying about something as a sign that things are slipping back into the vicious circle of GAD. The important thing to remember, as we mentioned at the start of this book, is that we are not aiming to remove all anxiety from your life – just the anxiety that isn't proportionate to the situation you are in. Anxiety and the adrenalin response that produces the physical symptoms of anxiety are normal.

Adrenalin serves a useful purpose and we need the anxiety response our body produces to keep us safe from harm, when the anxiety is relevant and at a realistic level to the situation we are facing. If we step out in front of a car, it is the adrenalin response that helps alert us to the danger and to jump back onto the pavement to keep us safe. Our aim in this book is to get your anxiety and your worries more in balance with the situations you are facing. The techniques that you have used have helped you to do that. There will be times when you get anxious and worried. There may be times when you slip into old patterns of worrying, especially if you have a big life event happening. The key thing is to recognise it and apply the techniques you have learned to stop the vicious circle in its tracks.

Having a relapse-prevention toolkit will help you to do just that. In this section we want to help you put together your own personalised helpful toolkit.

You can think of this section as a toolkit to help you to:

- Know what the early warning signs were when you were anxious or worried a lot before.

- Consider the things that may have kept you in that vicious circle, so you can spot them if they return: any negative anxious thoughts that you may have had; the things you avoided altogether, that you put off doing or over-prepared for because of how you were feeling; and any reassurance you sought from other key people in your life.

- Ensure you know how the worry management techniques helped you to feel better and the steps that you took to make them work. Keeping your worry management skills fresh using your toolkit means you will remember what to do should you need them again.

- Know where to get further help and support in the future should you need it.

Being compassionate to yourself when you have a lapse in worrying again is important. This means, don't expect to be worry-free every day; that isn't going to happen. And don't worry that any symptoms you may have of anxiety are a sign that you are back to square one. It is simply a sign that your body is working correctly and producing adrenalin. If you are feeling anxious again regularly, or are finding that you are having lots of hypothetical worries, feeling tense or having practical worries that you are not taking the action you need to solve the problem more days than not – you have the techniques and skills to manage this again, just like you have done this time.

Remember, you have the experience of managing your own anxiety and worry successfully using the worry management techniques. A lapse does not mean that you have relapsed.

The best thing to do if you recognise that you have got into a pattern of worrying and feeling anxious is to put your worry management skills into action. Breaking the pattern before it takes hold will help again, just like it did before. You have the experience of using the techniques to help yourself successfully and you can do so again should you ever need them.

Just like any new skill, worry management requires regular practice. As part of your relapse-prevention toolkit we will create a wellbeing action plan. Putting this into action reduces the likelihood of the vicious circle forming again. It also gives you confidence that you can spot any red flags indicating that your worry and anxiety is taking hold, and take action again.

What is the difference between a lapse and a relapse?

A **lapse** is a brief return to feeling anxious and worrying, or changes in what you do as a result. A lapse at times is normal. As long as we put into practice the worry management techniques we have learned we can get back on track. A lapse can become a relapse if you allow it to take control of you. Worrying thoughts or seeing it as a sign of failure will contribute to this. The important thing is to see a lapse for what it is, just temporary. Don't let it make you give up doing things you need to do or act in other ways that can keep the vicious circle going. Don't give up. Just keep doing the things in this guide that have helped you before. Remember, feeling anxious and worrying is a part of everyday life and those feelings are normal and OK when they are in proportion to what is happening to us in our lives.

A **relapse** is when worrying, reassurance and avoidance behaviours creep back over a longer period of time. The vicious circle starts to spiral again, making you feel worse and you find that those worries take over every day and affect what you are doing as a result. A relapse is not a total setback. You have the skills and techniques that helped before to help you again, and you know it worked. The key thing is to notice early warning signs and to put into action your worry management techniques again that helped you before.

Early warning signs

Signs that it may be time to take action are if:

- you spend most of your days worrying and feeling anxious as a result;

- your worries and anxiety stick around more days than not;

- you notice that you are getting back to ways of thinking and doing that did not help or back-fired before.

This is when it is time to put your worry management skills back into action. Sometimes feeling anxious again may be triggered by a specific event that is happening in your life – we know that people with GAD often experience periods of worry and anxiety when facing a key life event – but there may not be a particular trigger.

Keeping to your wellbeing action plan for staying well means that if you do notice you are worrying or feeling anxious again you should spot it early and know what to do. Knowing when you have had periods of worry and anxiety in the past can also help you to plan ahead for things that may be happening in your life and put your techniques into action to help you first.

My early warning signs

Think about what symptoms you noticed first when you began to realise that your worry and anxiety had become a problem for you. What physical symptoms, what thoughts and what changes in what you did (or didn't do) happened as a result? If you have always been a worrier, think about a time when it was particularly problematic for you.

You may find it helpful to ask a relative, loved one or friend what they noticed first, as often people around us notice things before we may be aware of them. If they noticed any early signs – for example, avoiding things, being more irritable than usual, or problems in sleeping – add these in too.

We really encourage you to spend some time identifying these symptoms: they are your early warning signs for the future.

The ABC diagram below will help you. In it write:

A – the **physical symptoms** you noticed first when you were anxious;

B – the changes you noticed in **what you did** more or less of as a result;

C – any changes to the type of **thoughts** you had.

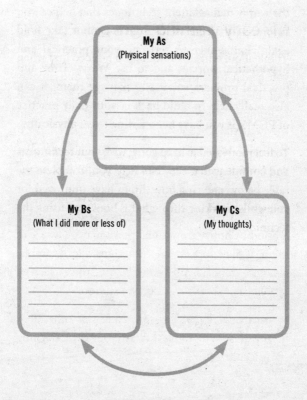

My As
(Physical sensations)

My Bs
(What I did more or less of)

My Cs
(My thoughts)

These are your red flag symptoms to look for in continuing to manage your worrying and anxiety. Having them every now and again is OK, but if you notice that you have difficulties in each of these areas and that a vicious circle is beginning to form you can take action using the techniques that you have learned. If you, or someone you share your plan with, spot signs that red flag symptoms are creeping back in, it is a good time to begin taking action. Use the worry management techniques that helped you before, so that the vicious circle cannot take hold again. Remember to separate your practical and hypothetical worries and to use Worry Time and practical problem solving to manage them. It can also really help to build back in your daily practice of PGMR if you have been feeling tense physically.

To feel motivated to keep going with your techniques and confident that they can help you, complete the table below, entering how things have improved for you whilst working through this book and using the techniques.

How things have improved since the start of treatment

What things are you now doing that you were not doing when you were worrying extensively and anxious?

List here any changes you have noticed as signs of things improving for you:

_____

_____

_____

_____

_____

_____

_____

_____

_____

_____

_____

_____

_____

_____

_____

_____

_____

List here the positive consequences of managing your
worry and anxiety and the improvements for you in
different areas of your life as a result.

Your work life

_____

_____

_____

_____

_____

Things around the home

_____

_____

_____

_____

_____

Your family life

_____

_____

_____

_____

_____

Your friendships

_____

_____

_____

_____

_____

Your social life

_____

_____

_____

_____

_____

The wellbeing action plan

The other really helpful strategy for your toolkit is to develop is a wellbeing action plan. Set some time aside as your **wellbeing day** each month (or weekly/ fortnightly if you can) to review the action plan and how you are feeling. This means you will hopefully pick up on your early warning signs of the vicious circle taking hold. It also means that you keep your worry management skills fresh by revisiting the treatment that helped and how it works.

My wellbeing action plan

Keeping check of my anxiety
Review date:
How have I been feeling this week/fortnight/month (delete as applicable)?   _____   _____   _____   _____   _____
Reading through early warning signs, have I had any that I am concerned about?   _____   _____   _____   _____

Have I got any signs of:	Yes	No
• Hypothetical worries during the day that are hard to let go of		
• Practical current worries that feel overwhelming to take any action about		
• Avoiding things due to being anxious		
• Putting things off		
• Over-preparing for things		
• Seeking reassurance from friends, colleagues or loved ones		
• Feeling tense or other physical symptoms of anxiety		

Do I need to take any action now to manage my worry and anxiety?

_____

If I need to take action, what technique(s) helped before that I can use to help again?

_____

_____

_____

_____

_____

If so, what do I need to do and when am I going to do it?

_____

_____

_____

_____

_____

If things are going well, what is it that has been helping me?

_____

_____

_____

_____

_____

Keeping my worry management skills fresh

What are the key stages of the Worry Time technique?

_____

_____

_____

_____

_____

What are the key stages of the practical problem-solving technique?

_____

_____

_____

_____

_____

What are the key stages of progressive muscle relaxation?

_____

_____

_____

_____

_____

Date of my next review day:

_____

Put this on my calendar or phone so I will see it as a reminder.

Is there still anything you would like to work on?

Sometimes there are areas that you might still want to see change in. These may be goals that you set at the start of treatment that you would like to work on further. Or perhaps they are other things that you would like to do, now that you are feeling less anxious and more able to manage your worry and anxiety.

If so what do you still want to do?

_____

_____

_____

_____

_____

How will you do it?

_____

_____

_____

_____

_____

When will you do it?

_____

_____

_____

_____

_____

Are there any resources you need to do it?

_____

_____

_____

_____

_____

What might get in the way of doing it and how can you overcome this?

_____

_____

_____

_____

_____

Top tips from others

Below are some tips from other people who have worked through the techniques in this book, and practitioners who have supported them in using them.

Top tip 1	'The best advice I can give would be that it is OK to feel anxious and not to worry if you worry sometimes! I no longer fear feeling this way and know I can manage what the future throws at me.'
Top tip 2	'Know your red flag early warning signs. Watch for times when you feel more stressed or when big things happen in your life. I shared my list with my wife and she sometimes notices before me that I am getting nervy again and reminds me to look through the book again and use the techniques.'
Top tip 3	'Use your wellbeing action plan even if you are feeling well. It really reminds you to look after yourself and to set aside time for it.'
Top tip 4	'Put your wellbeing day on the calendar each month in a coloured pen, so you know it is your review time. Or add a note to your mobile, or leave a Post-it Note on the fridge!'
Top tip 5	'Remember, it is doing the opposite that can often help. When I notice I don't feel like doing something, like going to see a friend, I make sure I still go. When I notice I am worrying sat in the chair, I get up and do something else.'

Top tip 6	'Focus on the present moment. If you notice that you are having worrying thoughts that are distracting you, the best thing to do is an activity that focuses your attention.'
Top tip 7	'Think about small changes you can make that add up to big changes you may still want to do. Think of the big change as like the end destination you put in your Sat Nav. Even when it feels far off, there are roads you can take to get nearer to where you want to be. Just make sure you are still heading in the right direction.'
Top tip 8	'Reflect on how far you have come.'
Top tip 9	'Don't get too focused on reviewing your mood, anxiety or worrying. Use your relapse-prevention toolkit as often as you need to, with a regular wellbeing day that you stick to. Remember that your anxiety will fluctuate up and down at times – that is normal and OK!'

Getting further help if you need it

Sometimes if you have put into place all the options you can, managing your anxiety and worry may still require additional support. Knowing where and how to get help is a good thing to have in your toolkit.

Where can I get more help?

Think of a supportive family member or friend, someone that you trust. Could you share this toolkit with them so they can help you watch for your red flag early warning signs?

They will then also know what you need to do to feel better. Write the name of someone you can identify as your toolkit supporter here:

....

Fill in your GP details here:

Surgery address:

....

....

....

....

Telephone number:

....

....

....

If you live in England and feel you would benefit from even more support you can look for the name of your local IAPT service and self-refer by contacting them, or ask your GP to refer you here:

http://www.iapt.nhs.uk/services/ [www.]

If you don't live in England, ask your GP what support may be available. You can also find private accredited therapists trained in CBT here:

http://www.cbtregisteruk.com/ [www.]

Congratulations!

You have come so far to reach this point, and we are delighted you stayed with the book and with us. Look what you have achieved as a result! Reflect on the progress you have made on the goals you set at the start. We know it may not have always been easy, and we cannot take any of the credit for you feeling better. That is all down to you – you alone are the reason! We just provided the tools to help you to help yourself. It is down to the work you did using worry management in your daily life.

The relapse-prevention section will help you to keep feeling this way. It will make sure you know when to put the tools back into action, should you ever need to. The book is always here should you need it. Be proud of what you have done.

In the next section we return to Graham and Sarah to hear how they used the worry management techniques to get well and stay well. You may have already read their stories earlier in the book. You may want to write your own story to add into it. This would be a lovely reminder of all the work you have done. Then, if you ever need to do more self-help, you can re-read it, knowing that you did it before and can do it again! Many people have found this a really helpful thing to do.

Others have also written themselves a short letter celebrating how much better they feel. Then they ask a friend or relative to post it back to them in three months' time. It becomes a surprise reminder of what they have accomplished and can do again if they ever need to. If a practitioner is supporting you, you could ask them to send the letter to you in three months' time.

We have also provided a further resources section at the back. This has blank copies of all the worksheets in this book so you can photocopy them as often as you need to or write in them as you are using the techniques in the future.

Good luck with your next steps and remember you have the skills to help yourself to feel better!

Marie and Paul

GRAHAM AND SARAH'S STORIES

You briefly met Sarah and Graham in Section 2. Here we give the full stories of how they used the interventions, along with examples of the worksheets they completed so you can look at these at any time during using the book.

Reading these examples of people who have used the techniques within this book can help in a range of ways:

- You can see how the techniques are carried out in action.

- You can see anything other people found difficult and how they overcame it.

- You can look at their worksheets to know how the intervention is carried out.

> - It can give hope that if it worked for them, it can work for you too.
>
> - If you get stuck at any point, you can read what someone else did.

Although Sarah and Graham's situations may be different to your own, the techniques that they used are the same ones you will use. This should help you to see how people carry out the techniques and what they do next. You can also come back to the stories and worksheets at any time if you are unsure what to do or how to complete the techniques.

Graham's story

> Graham, who you met in Section 2, was a 29-year-old salesman in a large company

when he began his worry management techniques. Graham had been promoted to the Team Leader for his section and enjoyed the sociable office environment. He had met his fiancée Emma there. Here, Graham tells his story about his experience of having GAD and his use of the Worry Time and PGMR techniques in particular.

"At first I didn't think that my worrying was a problem; I had always been a worrier. It was a family joke that I worried so much and had to plan things through to the last detail. I'd been like it since I was young. It was part of who I saw myself as: a worrier. I realised things had become a problem though and that my worrying had started to take over my life when I got engaged to Emma and we began planning our wedding in France where her parents live. I just couldn't switch off. Around the same time, I had been promoted at work, and my worrying just kept getting worse and worse. I was tense and irritable all the time and worried that there was something wrong with me. Emma wanted to book a break to France, to see her parents celebrate our engagement with them and start to get organised with planning the wedding. But I just couldn't face it and avoided talking about it or committing to dates to go. I felt pulled in so many directions and everything felt like it was too much. I worried about taking leave from work so shortly after being promoted and didn't think the team would do things properly if I wasn't there watching over them.

I spent most days with a headache and had so much work to do that Emma and I never spent any quality time together anymore. So a holiday was probably just what we needed but the thought of travelling and leaving work made me feel sick with worry. Things spiralled out of control. I knew Emma was getting frustrated with me; I was getting frustrated with myself too. It was like there was no respite from working and worrying. Even at night I never relaxed, in fact it seemed to get worse. I was always lost up in my head worrying and I knew I was lousy company. I would just get into a bout of worrying and not be able to stop. I would try and try to push the worries out of my mind. I would try to think about something else, but it didn't give me much respite and it was exhausting. It was really hard to concentrate.

It felt like I wasn't really living my life anymore; everything had to be planned in advance in minute detail and I just felt so overwhelmed with things that I stopped being able to focus on anything except work. I can see now I took on far too much responsibility for things, trying to make sure everything was under tight control. I had a team of 11 staff; but I was checking everything they did myself before releasing any budgets, reports or letters. I wanted to sign off everything they did first, which was an impossible task to set myself. It was exhausting. I was always first into the office and last to leave, normally with a big pile of work to take home and check through in the evening. I even started to doubt myself and worried that I may have missed something, so I would ask Emma to check as well. She had been at work all day too, so it didn't help our relationship to say the least.

I felt tense all the time, like a tightly wound spring, and I worried that I would snap and end up shouting at Emma or someone else. Emma said she didn't want to speak to me sometimes, as I just seemed so tense and on edge. Often in the evenings she would be watching the soaps upstairs and I would be downstairs going over data and reports and we would hardly speak. We used to be out all the time with friends at the weekend but we never went out anywhere anymore. Emma said she didn't mind staying in as it helped us save for the wedding, but deep down I think she did. At work, people talked about what great weekends they had had and all we had done was check over my team's work and watch TV. We didn't even go to the gym together anymore as I was always so exhausted, felt achy and had no time around work.

I knew Emma was really excited planning the wedding and desperately wanted to go over to her parents'. The whole thought of the trip to France, let alone the wedding itself, made me anxious: the money; the planning; inviting the right people; finding the right photographer; whether people could afford to come out to France and celebrate with us; if my family would be OK about us getting married there and not in our local church. I was so worried that things would go wrong and not be perfect for Emma. I wanted everything to be right for her. Normally I like to be the one to take on the responsibility of making sure things go right, but with the wedding planning I felt so out of my depth I avoided it completely! I know Emma must have been upset with me, but I used to feel sick at the thought of it and wandered around pretending it wasn't happening. I just couldn't get excited about it. Every time I thought about it I would try and push it out of my mind. It didn't work. I always had it in the back of my mind.

Things came to a head because I was worrying all the time and couldn't stop it, and I had such bad headaches that I was concerned that there was something physically wrong with me and kept asking Emma for reassurance that I wasn't physically ill or going crazy. I was exhausted and had headaches every day. I ached all over and just felt like all the life had been zapped out of me. I had stopped drinking alcohol completely as it made me feel more anxious and I had enough headaches without drinking. I didn't even drink coffee anymore. I went to the optician to be checked out to see if my eyesight was affecting my headaches. Everything was fine, but he did raise the fact that tension and stress can cause headaches like the ones I described and suggested I spoke to my GP if I thought that could be an issue for me. I hadn't realised being tense and worrying could affect you so much physically. Emma thought it might help to go and see the GP together and see if he could give me something to help. I knew there was a problem and that my anxiety was impacting on both of us, so I agreed.

When I walked into the surgery and was called in, the GP was a locum who I hadn't seen before. I didn't think he would take me seriously and worried he would think I was wasting his time. He asked me what the problem was; he listened to my list of physical symptoms and worries and asked if I had considered getting some help for my anxiety. I told him I wanted someone or something to take away this anxious feeling of dread that something awful and unknown was about to happen. He checked out my headaches too and from what I had described said he thought they were stress and tension related and that they would improve if my anxiety improved too. He explained that he thought that I would benefit from being assessed by the local Talk Therapy service to see what they could offer. I would have tried anything, but I wasn't a big talker so I wasn't sure if it was the right thing. I said I would give it a go anyway and I spoke to Emma on the way back in the car and she thought it was a good idea and worth finding out more about. I was worried about taking time off work, but I knew I needed to do something.

The Talk Therapy service sent me an assessment appointment, which was at my GP surgery about ten days later with a man called Tim. He asked me lots of questions about my anxiety and worry, in fact he got me to fill in a questionnaire about worry, which summed up exactly what I felt like! That made me feel a bit more normal as if they have questions like that then other people must get like this too. He explained about GAD and gave me some information to take away. I was a little daunted as I had barely enough time in the day as it was, let alone adding in more things to do, but Tim was encouraging and said it helped lots of other people and they could support me to use the techniques in a short phone call each week rather than me having to go into my GP surgery. I liked that idea, as I didn't have to take time off work or try and fit in travelling there, which was always stressful in the city traffic. It meant I could do the tasks in my own time and then take the call wherever I was. I was even able to login to a portal beforehand and fill in the measures they gave me each time and email my homework sheets over to Tim. It was really flexible.

The first thing he got me to do was to keep a diary of my worries for a week. I did laugh when he handed me just one sheet of paper with a diary on it – I could fill that in ten minutes, let alone a week! He asked me how many I felt I needed and then gave me some spare copies, and off I went to write down everything I worried about. He showed me how to see if they were hypothetical worries or practical ones, using the classifying tool. I found that the hardest bit, actually, as everything seemed practical and like it needed doing straight away. I worried about work, Emma, getting married, going away, planning things and my health. All of which seemed practical as they are about real things in my life. Tim had explained that practical worries were about things outside of me – practical problems where I could take action towards solving them at the time. Most other worries were hypothetical if there was no action that I could or should be taking at the time. It was so hard though as nearly everything seemed practical and I felt I needed to do something about it. I am glad he gave me the extra sheets; writing it down in black and white made me realise just how much of the day I worry [**a snapshot of Graham's Worry Diary is on page 132**]. Some things were hard to classify, even with Tim's explanation. Surely I should be worrying about the wedding and helping Emma plan, for example? I was surprised just how much I wrote down.

The following week I emailed my completed Worry Diary forms back to Tim and said in the email that I had struggled to classify something on it. He replied that we could discuss it at our next appointment. When he called me for the appointment we discussed the diary. He helped me to reclassify some of my worries in a really helpful way. He said that although the wedding is a real thing, if I was at work and should have been concentrating on a meeting but found myself worrying about the wedding instead, at that moment it became a hypothetical worry as there wasn't anything I could (or should) do about it then. I should have been focused on what was happening in the meeting, not lost up in my head worrying. That really helped me to see the difference and made it much easier to classify the others. Tim asked me to reflect on the diary and what I noticed. It helped me to see I spent a lot of time lost in my head worrying about hypothetical things and just how many hypothetical worries I was having. I also noticed I tended to have them at night as I was trying to get off to sleep or if I was sat in front of the TV not really watching it while Emma was watching the soaps.

Based on what I had written down and what we had discussed Tim then asked me which of the techniques I had read about did I think would help me? I was keen to try progressive muscle relaxation to see if it would help with my tension and irritability and also Worry Time. Tim agreed that both options would be good to help with my worrying and other symptoms. We made a plan for me to start with progressive muscle relaxation (PGMR) and then to begin using Worry Time after that.

I felt a bit silly practising the muscle relaxation at first with Tim. We went though it over the phone in our appointment and then I practised it at home every day at a set time. Tim had sent me a worksheet of muscle groups to tense and then to relax. It actually hurt a bit the first few times. I did notice though that I started to look forward to it each evening. It took about 15 minutes to work through, starting from my feet up to my forehead. Emma sat and did it with me sometimes too, which was nice. I didn't notice much effect though after a week and said to Tim I wasn't sure if it was working. Tim explained it can take a few weeks of practice for my muscles to learn to let go of the tension I carry round and to not hold on to the tension each time I got anxious. He recommended that I keep practising it each day at my set time for at least a month. I am really glad I kept going.

Date & Time	Situation (where you are, what you are doing and what is going on around you)	Your Worry (e.g. 'What if.......')	How anxious do you feel on a 0–10 scale? (0–not at all anxious, 10–the most anxious you have ever been)	Practical (P) or Hypothetical (H)? (tick the column below)	
				P	H
Monday 6th March	Sat at home having breakfast with Emma	What if we are late for work? What if Matthew rings in sick and the data run is late?	7		x
//	At work, my boss comes over to my desk	What if I have done something wrong?	8		x
//	On the way home from work with Emma talking about getting married	What if I can't cope with the wedding?	6		x?

//	Trying to drop off to sleep, in bed. Emma out at yoga	What if Emma has an accident? I should have taken her.	7	x
7th March	In meeting at work presenting	What if the figures are wrong and I haven't checked them enough?	8	x?
//	Sat at my desk, really bad headache	I am sure there is something wrong with me. What if I have a brain tumour or something else going on that the GP hasn't noticed?	7	x
//	Working at home checking emails	What if I have missed something important?	8	x
//	Sat in bed, Emma asleep	What if Emma gets sick of me and leaves?	9	x

An excerpt from Graham's worry diary

What I did notice, well Emma noticed first to be honest, was that I was complaining about headaches much less and taking fewer painkillers. That was a good sign for sure. I also began to notice that when I got anxious about things I clenched my jaw and teeth together and how noticing when I was doing it and letting it go felt so much nicer and actually made me feel a bit calmer. Over time, I noticed when I was tensing up, particularly at work or in stressful situations, and I was able to let it go. Just doing that really helped me to feel less anxious too. I would really recommend progressive muscle relaxation (PGMR). The time it takes is minimal and it has done so much for the physical symptoms of GAD I had. I have kept up practising it and find it so useful.

I had told Tim that I wasn't convinced that Worry Time would work for me as there was no way I could switch off my worries until the evening with the amount of them I was having and that I had tried to block them out before but it had only led to more of them! Tim said he thought that it would be helpful to try it and explained that Worry Time had a way of helping to postpone worry that was different to the method I tried to block worry out. He explained that worries distract you from what you are doing so you are not aware of what is going on around you in the present moment. He explained that worry was a bit like a switch that turned your attention off the present and that if you refocused on the present moment and really paid attention to what was going on around you and the task that you are doing, the switch could equally turn off your worry. I thought it was worth a try and although I had some reservations, I agreed to set aside an hour at 8pm each evening after dinner to have as my Worry Time. It felt strange setting aside that time and initially I was concerned that my work would build up and up. Emma said she would make dinner and load the dishwasher each evening, then take our dog Ben out so I had the house to myself. I didn't know how I would fit all my worries into an hour, but I was willing to give it a go and liked the idea of being more in touch with things and focused on the present.

I tried it. I wrote down all the worries I had in my phone notebook during the day and then refocused my attention on the present. It was really hard to do sometimes. I would be lying if I said it was easy trying to switch off some of my worries, especially ones about Emma or the wedding. I found some worries kept coming back and sometimes the anxiety was so high it was hard to refocus. But I found just letting the worries come back and writing them down again, then doing another task was helpful. What I found worked well at work was to get up from whatever I was doing and either have a conversation with one of my team or go outside and notice the sights, sounds or smells and really pay attention, then come back to what I was doing. My team often had important questions or things they needed to hand over to me, so going to speak to them meant that I would have to pay attention to what they asked me or what they told me. At night, I didn't want to use my phone as I found the screen hard to see when my contact lenses were out and I didn't want keep waking Emma up with the bright screen, so I kept a worry list and pen at the side of the bed. I then tried to refocus on sleeping by noticing the feel of the covers and turning the pillow over to the cold side.

When it came around to the actual Worry Time each day, I found it hard to make myself worry for that long! Not what I was expecting at all. I didn't feel particularly anxious when I had the Worry Time hour and I didn't find the time was full at all, as most of my worries had already passed and didn't mean anything by then. Worrying Emma would be late in from work was irrelevant at 8pm when we had just eaten dinner together and she had been home for a few hours. I found that rather than me worrying non-stop and not having enough time, actually within a few sessions with Tim I felt much more in control of my worrying during the day. It wasn't always easy, especially when things happened at work or there were wedding things to plan, but I tried to get involved as much as I could with planning, which made Emma happier. Because I knew I had my Worry Time I knew I could worry as much as I needed to later in the day rather than in the moment. It was hard to refocus sometimes and I found carrying round a crossword book helped me. I would sometimes get it out after I had written down my worry and use that as a way of refocusing my attention onto a task. I have become very good at crosswords!

Tim was really pleased with my progress, as was I. OK, so it didn't suddenly stop me worrying; it took time and actually I do still worry every now and again, but everyone does. Now I don't do it as much and I feel more in control of what I do worry about and when. I cannot believe what a difference using PGMR and Worry Time has made to my life and now I feel that I am actually really living my life, not just coasting through it. Everything seems much brighter and better. I didn't realise just how not in touch with things I was. Looking back, I was always a worrier and I think it stopped me living life to the full. This is like a new beginning and I could not be happier. Everything is OK at work too. I have stopped being such a control freak and the team re-late so much better to me now too. Mark [one of the team] even commented that because I seemed so stressed it had made them stressed and they were so fearful of making mistakes and of my reaction that they had probably made more than normal! I was so shocked. We now have a team drink each week and are much more relaxed. I delegate much more and have an agreement with Emma that I don't bring work home unless it is essential and that even then we both switch off our laptops at 7pm and enjoy cooking together and then watching TV snuggled up on the sofa! I feel I have got my life back and Emma and I are so happy! We went to France and decided to plan the wedding for the following summer to give us lots of time to get things how we both wanted them. I even started a wedding blog with Emma! It was great fun planning. I should invite Tim to the wedding!**"**

Introducing Sarah's story

"It was a family joke that I was a worrier, just like my mother before me. I hated how much I worried but couldn't imagine not worrying and thought if I stopped that things would go catastrophically wrong somehow. Things built to a peak though when my husband Grant was made redundant. I was so worried that we would lose our lovely home and not be able to enjoy our life together when he retired. I also worried about him finding a new job at his age.

Our daughters Olivia and Emily were my life and I found it really hard when they both went off to university. You hear such awful things about students and drinking and people taking advantage of them that I tried to convince them to go to the local university. Probably like most girls their age though they wanted to spread their wings and chose one four hours' drive away from us. I was so proud of them; they are not like me at all, they are so outgoing and brave; but I was so anxious about them being there alone without me nearby and spent hours a day worrying about them or that something would happen to them on a night out in the big city. A city is a lot different from the little village we live in. How would they adapt? I dreaded hearing where they were going and what they were doing, yet I always asked and made sure they told me, as I had to know so I could check out the places online to see if I thought they would be safe. I made them ring me when they got in from parties or nights out to tell me they were safe, much to Grant's irritation at the phone ringing at all hours and probably their embarrassment at having an over-anxious over-controlling mum like me. Not 'cool' as they would tell me often.

I liked to be the one who controlled our finances and money and hated the idea of Grant doing it and things going wrong. I have to admit, though, I wasn't very good at it, even though I thought it was better for me to do it. I would spend ages researching the best options for our money and worried about choosing the wrong thing. I would repeatedly run everything past Grant for his opinion, but then not actually get round to doing it in time. Like when our credit card was coming to the end of its interest-free fixed rate period. I spent hours looking at other options and fretting about which would be the best and in the end our card came to the end of the time and we ended up with a hefty interest rate charge. Grant, as you can imagine, wasn't exactly pleased. I would just get paralysed with decisions and then put them off.

Grant had applied for a few jobs but had not got anything and it kept me awake at night worrying about what would happen. I knew that we would be OK for a while as he had got a good redundancy package, but what then? What if he didn't get another job and all our plans for life when he retired went out of the window? I think the combination of the girls going to university and the worry and stress about our finances, made everything reach a peak. I knew I was getting more and more tense and irritable and I wasn't easy to live with. Grant was patient, but I could tell even he was reaching his limits. Especially with things like the credit card and our needing to re-mortgage soon, which would be challenging with him having been made redundant.

Things came to a real head when the girls had mentioned they were going to a party their student union had arranged outside of the city, somewhere they had not been before, and that they would be back in very late as they had to get mini-buses there. On that same night, Grant and I had tickets to go and see a show in London that he had bought me for my birthday. I was really worried about going and the cost, even though the tickets had already been paid for. Grant had booked a lovely meal before the show and wanted us to have a really nice and romantic night away and to put our worries and stresses from the last few months to one side for the evening and enjoy ourselves. I was worried that the girls would get too drunk or that someone might spike their drink, or that they wouldn't get home safely. I mean, who was driving the mini-bus? Would they be drinking too before driving?

Or would they lose their way? Having a group of students in the bus would be really distracting for the driver. They could have an accident, for example. My head was spinning and not really focused as Grant and I packed to go to London.

Over the meal, which was in a beautiful restaurant. Grant said I hadn't spoke about anything but the girls and if they would be OK and that I must trust them more and have faith that they were sensible. I know he wanted a night off from me wittering and the stress of him looking for a job but I couldn't switch off. Even throughout the show, I was checking my mobile phone constantly and not really concentrating. It was a show I had gone on and on to Grant about how much I wanted to see, and I knew it wasn't really his thing, so I felt awful for doing it, but I didn't want to miss a call or text with my phone on silent. I don't even remember much of the show or even what I ate at the meal and what it tasted like, that's how bad things were. Instead of our lovely night away together I was distracted and anxious and could not sleep until the girls had rung to let me know they were back safely. That was 5am. We had to be up at 9am for breakfast and to meet some friends we had arranged to have brunch with across the other side of London. Grant didn't complain or argue with me about it that night, but I knew he was disappointed (and so was I) that I hadn't been able to switch off. I was fine over lunch with our friends Gemma and Ben as I knew the girls were OK, and as we were eating at their house we had just brought a nice bottle of wine and flowers, so I wasn't too worried about how much we had spent over the weekend.

When we got home, I said to Grant that I knew I had to deal with my anxiety and that I didn't want to be like that anymore. He looked so relieved to hear me say it and said he and the girls had planned to sit down with me and have the exact same conversation that weekend. I am glad I had plucked up the courage to speak to him first. I hated knowing that they had been talking about me and worrying about me and how much I was worrying. I didn't sleep well that night either, wondering about what I should do and what would happen when I did. I felt like if I went to see the GP he would say I was a silly old fool and that is exactly what I felt like. I know in reality that he would never say such a thing, but I couldn't help but imagine he would be thinking it. I was.

The next day Grant called me over to the computer. He had found a service that you could self-refer to that dealt with anxiety. Their website had people who had used the service talking about their experiences and one of them was someone who worried all the time, just like me. You could ring them and book in for an assessment, so I did. Right there and then. Grant actually high-fived me when I came off the phone! They had asked me a few questions and booked me in for an assessment at their office base on the local industrial estate a week later.

The assessment was fine. The lady I saw, Karen, was really warm and put me at ease. She had been specifically trained to work with people like me who were anxious. It only took about 45 minutes in total and I felt like I had got so much off my chest. I hadn't noticed before how much it was affecting me physically and affecting what I was doing. The questions she asked really linked everything together. She asked me about taking my own life, which I had never considered and came as a bit of a surprise, but she said that they ask that with every person every time they are seen. Overall, it was great. I felt better just speaking to someone who understood. She explained how all the areas were linked and gave me some information about Generalised Anxiety Disorder and worry. It was like reading my autobiography! It was me to a T. It had various things that could help me to manage my worry better instead of it taking over my whole life, like it felt at the time. I was so pleased to read that others felt like this too and that I wasn't going crazy (and Karen had not told me I was either and had explained that many, many people experience this). That was such a relief.

I had to wait a couple of weeks for treatment to start with Karen. It was definitely worth the wait though. We used the Worry Time technique to manage the worries that popped into my mind that I couldn't take any action on at the time I was worrying about them, or didn't need to take at that point as my attention should have been elsewhere. It really helped. I could actually sleep while the girls were on nights out, and because Karen had explained about the role of reassurance seeking, I realised that asking them when they would be back when they were going out was just making me feel more anxious if they didn't contact me at that exact time. I also realised I sought a lot of reassurance from Grant too. Showing him the self-help book that I was using with Karen for him to learn more about it was a really good idea that she suggested. Grant looked through it and said that he recognised that he gave me a lot of reassurance and that it could be keeping me caught in that vicious circle. He learned that when he answered all of my worries and gave me reassurance or made decisions for me, it didn't actually help us in the long term. It just made me worse and seek more reassurance from him, which he even admitted was irritating! Something he had not really said before. So we talked about it and he stopped! Despite my best efforts sometimes to get him to do it, he stuck to the 'once and factually accurate responses only' suggestion that Karen gave. If I asked the same thing again, he would just simply say he wasn't going to respond to me as it was giving me reassurance. How irritating but effective. It became a bit of a standing joke between us! Worry Time and reducing the reassurance that I sought was so helpful and made me feel like I could manage to control my worries rather than them controlling me. I also noticed Grant and I were beginning to argue less as a result and being more open with each other.

I think the thing that really stood out, though, was using practical problem solving. It seemed common sense, but it was something I really struggled to do. I could sit for hours and worry about hypothetical worries before using Worry Time, but when it was a practical worry that I actually should do something about, like the credit card issue, I didn't manage to get it done and sort it effectively. I noted on my Worry Diary that I was worrying about contacting our bank and explaining about Grant's job. I had to arrange for us to switch to a different bank account that didn't have a monthly charge while we got back on our feet. I had just put it off and off, just like the credit card. I still had not dealt with that either, so we had a hefty monthly payment we could ill-afford.

I had a support session with Karen and the practical worries came up. We spoke about how I would procrastinate and spend lots of time searching and worrying but then not take the action I needed to take. Karen helped me to see that with practical worries that did need action taking at the time I was worrying about them, I needed to deal with them and not let them wait. Unlike hypothetical worries, they could not be dealt with using Worry Time, as they did need me to deal with them by the required time. With Karen, I learned how to use the technique in the book to turn the practical worry into a clear, time-limited problem that can be solved. For example, my worry 'What if the bank won't let us change accounts?' was not clear and specific enough. So we changed this into 'I need to speak to the bank about the possibility of an account without a monthly use charge by the end of next week so I don't get charged again.'

Sarah's Problem Solving Worksheet Excerpt

My current practical problem is:

I need to speak to the bank about changing accounts to one without a monthly usage charge, before the next charge is put on at the end of next week.

Proposed Solutions	Strengths	Weaknesses	Ranking
Ignore it and get charged.	I don't have to deal with it.	We can't afford to pay a £24 charge each month for the benefits of the account that we no longer use such as travel insurance and the like.	3
Ring the bank and book an appointment.	Seems sensible and easy, talking over the phone may be less embarrassing and intimidating.	Have to find the number and deal with the irritating automated system. I may not get an appointment before next week or speak to someone who understands the situation we are in. Not very personal.	2
Go to the bank and request to speak to someone at the local branch.	It sorts the situation there and then (hopefully). I can have all our paperwork with me. I can look at the other account options while I am waiting as they have leaflets on display.	None, really. A little anxious people will know us, as it is a small village, but people know our situation anyway and I get on well with them in the branch and have been there since I was a teenager.	1

I could then come up with solutions to try and solve the problem. I even got to suggest just ignoring it! But the advantages and disadvantages of that were plain to see – that was the way things had been before and it didn't work out well! Ranking the solutions helped me to not jump onto what seemed the easiest thing to do by phoning them. Actually, I don't think that was the best thing when you looked at it; going into the branch was much better. So I did! And . . . they were great. I even got a cup of tea. It was helpful to hear that they thought we manage our account well and they were not concerned at the moment as Grant's redundancy pay-out meant our account was healthy. They let us move from the benefit-plus account to an everyday current account and also discussed with us moving our current credit card, which had a high rate, to their current one, which had a 0% rate for balance transfers. That way we didn't need to spend a chunk of the redundancy money paying off the card or have a large interest payment each month, which certainly gave us more wiggle room. By the end of the 12 months, hopefully Grant would have found work, or I would go back and do some teaching. Either way, it felt like a huge weight had been lifted from my shoulders. We also put a chunk of the redundancy payment into a high interest account so that we got a better return (and it meant we could not dip into it when we didn't need to), which should help it to last longer and go further. I really don't think I would have done it without using the problem solving steps with Karen.

I do still worry, it is natural, but I feel like I control it now, not the other way round. Worrying is ok if it leads to me taking the action I need to take on practical things and doesn't take over everything. Of course, like any mum, I worry about the girls and like to know where they are going for safety reasons, but they are adults now and I am not dogmatic about it and they no longer have to check in when they get home. Grant and I argue much less and he trusts me to do things when we discuss them and I even let him take over some of the household things and bills and don't check up whether he has done them. It hasn't been easy. There were a couple of times when I thought it wasn't working and nearly gave up. I am so glad I didn't. It does work, it has really helped and now the girls want to come home during the holidays and spend time with us as a family, not avoid coming home or telling me things. They seem much more open with me now about what they get up to at uni, although sometimes I wish they weren't! I am so glad they are having a great time and enjoying life; so is Grant. He hasn't found work yet, but has taken up some enjoyable voluntary work which will look good on his CV. He has an interview next week for a post he really wants and is really experienced in, so fingers crossed. What will be, will be, and whatever comes our way we will manage it together as a family. We are even pushing the boat out and having a nice family break at Christmas in a cottage on the coast. We are really looking forward to that. If the worst comes to the worst and Grant doesn't find work in the next year we are going to downsize and that will mean we will be comfortable for much longer.

Life is always challenging and I think I will always be a 'worrier'. It is part of who I am. It is just no longer the only thing I do! Now I problem solve and am productive and proactive. **"**

FURTHER RESOURCES

My goals for feeling better

Goal 1: ....

Longer term things I can do to work towards this goal over the next six months or so.

_____

_____

_____

Things that I can do towards this goal in the next month.

_____

_____

_____

Things I can do towards this goal in the next couple of weeks.

_____

_____

_____

Goal 2: ....

Longer term things I can do to work towards this goal over the next six months or so.

_____

_____

_____

Things that I can do towards this goal in the next month.

_____

_____

_____

Things I can do towards this goal in the next couple of weeks.

_____

_____

_____

Goal 3: ....

Longer term things I can do to work towards this goal over the next six months or so.

_____

_____

_____

Things that I can do towards this goal in the next month.

_____

_____

_____

Things I can do towards this goal in the next couple of weeks.

_____

_____

_____

My goals for feeling better

Goal 1:......................................

Longer term things I can do to work towards this goal over the next six months or so.

_____

_____

_____

Things that I can do towards this goal in the next month.

_____

_____

_____

Things I can do towards this goal in the next couple of weeks.

_____

_____

_____

Goal 2: ....

Longer term things I can do to work towards this goal over the next six months or so.

_____

_____

_____

Things that I can do towards this goal in the next month.

_____

_____

_____

Things I can do towards this goal in the next couple of weeks.

_____

_____

_____

Goal 3: ....

Longer term things I can do to work towards this goal over the next six months or so.

_____

_____

_____

Things that I can do towards this goal in the next month.

_____

_____

_____

Things I can do towards this goal in the next couple of weeks.

_____

_____

_____

My goals for feeling better

Goal 1: ....

Longer term things I can do to work towards this goal over the next six months or so.

_____

_____

_____

Things that I can do towards this goal in the next month.

_____

_____

_____

Things I can do towards this goal in the next couple of weeks.

_____

_____

_____

Goal 2: ....

Longer term things I can do to work towards this goal over the next six months or so.

Things that I can do towards this goal in the next month.

Things I can do towards this goal in the next couple of weeks.

Goal 3: ....

Longer term things I can do to work towards this goal over the next six months or so.

_____

_____

_____

Things that I can do towards this goal in the next month.

_____

_____

_____

Things I can do towards this goal in the next couple of weeks.

_____

_____

_____

Rating my goals

Goal 1: ....Today's date...................

I can do this now (circle a number):

0	1	2	3	4	5	6
Not at all		Occasionally		Often		Any time

One month re-rating (Today's date...................)
(circle a number):

0	1	2	3	4	5	6
Not at all		Occasionally		Often		Any time

Two month re-rating (Today's date...................)
(circle a number):

0	1	2	3	4	5	6
Not at all		Occasionally		Often		Any time

Three month re-rating (Today's date................)
(circle a number):

0	1	2	3	4	5	6
Not at all		Occasionally		Often		Any time

Goal 2:.................Today's date....................

I can do this now (circle a number):

0	1	2	3	4	5	6
Not at all		Occasionally		Often		Any time

One month re-rating (Today's date....................)
(circle a number):

0	1	2	3	4	5	6
Not at all		Occasionally		Often		Any time

Two month re-rating (Today's date....................)
(circle a number):

0	1	2	3	4	5	6
Not at all		Occasionally		Often		Any time

Three month re-rating (Today's date.................)
(circle a number):

0	1	2	3	4	5	6
Not at all		Occasionally		Often		Any time

Goal 3:...............Today's date...................

I can do this now (circle a number):

0	1	2	3	4	5	6
Not at all		Occasionally		Often		Any time

One month re-rating (Today's date...................)
(circle a number):

0	1	2	3	4	5	6
Not at all		Occasionally		Often		Any time

Two month re-rating (Today's date...................)
(circle a number):

0	1	2	3	4	5	6
Not at all		Occasionally		Often		Any time

Three month re-rating (Today's date................)
(circle a number):

0	1	2	3	4	5	6
Not at all		Occasionally		Often		Any time

Rating my goals

Goal 1: ....Today's date...................

I can do this now (circle a number):

0	1	2	3	4	5	6
Not at all		Occasionally		Often		Any time

One month re-rating (Today's date...................)
(circle a number):

0	1	2	3	4	5	6
Not at all		Occasionally		Often		Any time

Two month re-rating (Today's date...................)
(circle a number):

0	1	2	3	4	5	6
Not at all		Occasionally		Often		Any time

Three month re-rating (Today's date................)
(circle a number):

0	1	2	3	4	5	6
Not at all		Occasionally		Often		Any time

Goal 2:...............Today's date...................

I can do this now (circle a number):

0	1	2	3	4	5	6
Not at all		Occasionally		Often		Any time

One month re-rating (Today's date...................)
(circle a number):

0	1	2	3	4	5	6
Not at all		Occasionally		Often		Any time

Two month re-rating (Today's date...................)
(circle a number):

0	1	2	3	4	5	6
Not at all		Occasionally		Often		Any time

Three month re-rating (Today's date................)
(circle a number):

0	1	2	3	4	5	6
Not at all		Occasionally		Often		Any time

Goal 3:................Today's date....................

I can do this now (circle a number):

0	1	2	3	4	5	6
Not at all		Occasionally		Often		Any time

One month re-rating (Today's date...................)
(circle a number):

0	1	2	3	4	5	6
Not at all		Occasionally		Often		Any time

Two month re-rating (Today's date...................)
(circle a number):

0	1	2	3	4	5	6
Not at all		Occasionally		Often		Any time

Three month re-rating (Today's date.................)
(circle a number):

0	1	2	3	4	5	6
Not at all		Occasionally		Often		Any time

Rating my goals

Goal 1: ....Today's date...................

I can do this now (circle a number):

0	1	2	3	4	5	6
Not at all		Occasionally		Often		Any time

One month re-rating (Today's date...................)
(circle a number):

0	1	2	3	4	5	6
Not at all		Occasionally		Often		Any time

Two month re-rating (Today's date...................)
(circle a number):

0	1	2	3	4	5	6
Not at all		Occasionally		Often		Any time

Three month re-rating (Today's date...............)
(circle a number):

0	1	2	3	4	5	6
Not at all		Occasionally		Often		Any time

Goal 2:...............Today's date...................

I can do this now (circle a number):

0	1	2	3	4	5	6
Not at all		Occasionally		Often		Any time

One month re-rating (Today's date...................)
(circle a number):

0	1	2	3	4	5	6
Not at all		Occasionally		Often		Any time

Two month re-rating (Today's date...................)
(circle a number):

0	1	2	3	4	5	6
Not at all		Occasionally		Often		Any time

Three month re-rating (Today's date................)
(circle a number):

0	1	2	3	4	5	6
Not at all		Occasionally		Often		Any time

Goal 3:...............Today's date...................

I can do this now (circle a number):

0	1	2	3	4	5	6
Not at all		Occasionally		Often		Any time

One month re-rating (Today's date...................)
(circle a number):

0	1	2	3	4	5	6
Not at all		Occasionally		Often		Any time

Two month re-rating (Today's date...................)
(circle a number):

0	1	2	3	4	5	6
Not at all		Occasionally		Often		Any time

Three month re-rating (Today's date...............)
(circle a number):

0	1	2	3	4	5	6
Not at all		Occasionally		Often		Any time

Worry Diary Table

Date & Time	Situation (where you are, what you are doing and what is going on around you)	Your Worry (e.g. 'What if......')	How anxious do you feel on a 0–10 scale? (0–not at all anxious, 10–the most anxious you have ever been)	Practical (P) or Hypothetical (H)? (tick the column below) P	H

Worry Diary Table

Date & Time	Situation (where you are, what you are doing and what is going on around you)	Your Worry (e.g. 'What if.......')	How anxious do you feel on a 0–10 scale? (0–not at all anxious, 10–the most anxious you have ever been)	Practical (P) or Hypothetical (H)? (tick the column below)	
				P	H

Worry Diary Table

Date & Time	Situation (where you are, what you are doing and what is going on around you)	Your Worry (e.g. 'What if.......')	How anxious do you feel on a 0–10 scale? (0–not at all anxious, 10–the most anxious you have ever been)	Practical (P) or Hypothetical (H)? (tick the column below)	
				P	H

Worry Diary Table

Date & Time	Situation (where you are, what you are doing and what is going on around you)	Your Worry (e.g. 'What if.......')	How anxious do you feel on a 0–10 scale? (0–not at all anxious, 10–the most anxious you have ever been)	Practical (P) or Hypothetical (H)? (tick the column below) P	H

Worry Diary Table

Date & Time	Situation (where you are, what you are doing and what is going on around you)	Your Worry (e.g. 'What if.......')	How anxious do you feel on a 0–10 scale? (0–not at all anxious, 10–the most anxious you have ever been)	Practical (P) or Hypothetical (H)? (tick the column below)	
				P	H

Worry Diary Table

Date & Time	Situation (where you are, what you are doing and what is going on around you)	Your Worry (e.g. 'What if.......')	How anxious do you feel on a 0–10 scale? (0–not at all anxious, 10–the most anxious you have ever been)	Practical (P) or Hypothetical (H)? (tick the column below) P	H

Behaviours
(Things you have noticed
you are avoiding, or doing
more of as a result of how
your are feeling.)

_____

_____

_____

_____

Thoughts
(Changes in your thinking.
Try to write them as the
specific thoughts that went
through your mind.)

_____

_____

_____

_____

Physical
(Physical changes
you have noticed.)

_____

_____

_____

_____

Behaviours
(Things you have noticed
you are avoiding, or doing
more of as a result of how
your are feeling.)

_____
_____
_____
_____

Thoughts
(Changes in your thinking.
Try to write them as the
specific thoughts that went
through your mind.)

_____
_____
_____
_____

Physical
(Physical changes
you have noticed.)

_____
_____
_____
_____

My hypothetical worries today

My Hypothetical Worries Today	
My scheduled Worry Time is:_____am/pm for:_____mins	
My Worry:	To refocus on the present moment I am now going to:
e.g. What if I have made a mistake at work?	e.g. Put the radio on and cook dinner (spaghetti) and notice the lovely smells and sing along!

My hypothetical worries today

My Hypothetical Worries Today	
My scheduled Worry Time is:_____am/pm for:_____mins	
My Worry:	To refocus on the present moment I am now going to:
e.g. What if I have made a mistake at work?	e.g. Put the radio on and cook dinner (spaghetti) and notice the lovely smells and sing along!

My hypothetical worries today

My Hypothetical Worries Today	
My scheduled Worry Time is:_____am/pm for:_____mins	
My Worry:	To refocus on the present moment I am now going to:
e.g. What if I have made a mistake at work?	e.g. Put the radio on and cook dinner (spaghetti) and notice the lovely smells and sing along!

My hypothetical worries today

My Hypothetical Worries Today	
My scheduled Worry Time is:_____am/pm for:_____mins	
My Worry:	To refocus on the present moment I am now going to:
e.g. What if I have made a mistake at work?	e.g. Put the radio on and cook dinner (spaghetti) and notice the lovely smells and sing along!

Worksheet A

My current practical problem is:

Proposed Solutions	Strengths	Weaknesses	Ranking

Worksheet A

My current practical problem is:

Proposed Solutions	Strengths	Weaknesses	Ranking

Worksheet A

My current practical problem is:

Proposed Solutions	Strengths	Weaknesses	Ranking

Worksheet A

My current practical problem is:

Proposed Solutions	Strengths	Weaknesses	Ranking

Worksheet B

Putting the solution into action:	Reviewing the outcome:
What are you going to do?	How did it go?
When are you going to do it?	Has it solved the problem sufficiently?
Where are you going to do it?	If not go back to your list of ranked solutions on Worksheet A and put the next one into action, planning – on a new Worksheet B – what you are going to do and when you are going to do it.

Is there anyone you need with you?

Are there any things you need to do first?

Is there anything that might get in the way of your plan?
What can you do to overcome these obstacles?

If it went to plan and solved the problem, great! What have you learned from doing it that you can apply to the next practical problem that you have?

Worksheet B

Putting the solution into action:	Reviewing the outcome:
What are you going to do?	How did it go?
When are you going to do it?	Has it solved the problem sufficiently?
Where are you going to do it?	If not go back to your list of ranked solutions on Worksheet A and put the next one into action, planning – on a new Worksheet B – what you are going to do and when you are going to do it.

Is there anyone you need with you?

Are there any things you need to do first?

Is there anything that might get in the way of your plan?
What can you do to overcome these obstacles?

If it went to plan and solved the problem, great! What
have you learned from doing it that you can apply to the
next practical problem that you have?

Worksheet B

Putting the solution into action:	Reviewing the outcome:
What are you going to do?	How did it go?
When are you going to do it?	Has it solved the problem sufficiently?
Where are you going to do it?	If not go back to your list of ranked solutions on **Worksheet A** and put the next one into action, planning – on a new **Worksheet B** – what you are going to do and when you are going to do it.

Is there anyone you need with you?

Are there any things you need to do first?

Is there anything that might get in the way of your plan?
What can you do to overcome these obstacles?

If it went to plan and solved the problem, great! What have you learned from doing it that you can apply to the next practical problem that you have?

Worksheet B

Putting the solution into action:	Reviewing the outcome:
What are you going to do?	How did it go?
When are you going to do it?	Has it solved the problem sufficiently?
Where are you going to do it?	If not go back to your list of ranked solutions on **Worksheet A** and put the next one into action, planning – on a new **Worksheet B** – what you are going to do and when you are going to do it.

Is there anyone you need with you?

Are there any things you need to do first?

Is there anything that might get in the way of your plan? What can you do to overcome these obstacles?

If it went to plan and solved the problem, great! What have you learned from doing it that you can apply to the next practical problem that you have?

How things have improved since the start of treatment

What things are you now doing that you were not doing when you were worrying extensively and anxious?

List here any changes you have noticed as signs of things improving for you:

_____

_____

_____

_____

_____

_____

_____

_____

_____

_____

_____

_____

_____

_____

_____

List here the positive consequences of managing your worry and anxiety and the improvements for you in different areas of your life as a result.

Your work life

_____

_____

_____

_____

_____

Things around the home

_____

_____

_____

_____

_____

Your family life

_____

_____

_____

_____

_____

Your friendships

_____

_____

_____

_____

_____

Your social life

_____

_____

_____

_____

_____

How things have improved since the start of treatment

What things are you now doing that you were not doing when you were worrying extensively and anxious?

List here any changes you have noticed as signs of things improving for you:

_____

_____

_____

_____

_____

_____

_____

_____

_____

_____

_____

_____

_____

_____

_____

List here the positive consequences of managing your worry and anxiety and the improvements for you in different areas of your life as a result.

Your work life

_____

_____

_____

_____

_____

Things around the home

_____

_____

_____

_____

_____

Your family life

_____

_____

_____

_____

_____

Your friendships

_____

_____

_____

_____

_____

Your social life

_____

_____

_____

_____

_____

How things have improved since the start of treatment

What things are you now doing that you were not doing when you were worrying extensively and anxious?

List here any changes you have noticed as signs of things improving for you:

_____

_____

_____

_____

_____

_____

_____

_____

_____

_____

_____

_____

_____

_____

_____

List here the positive consequences of managing your
worry and anxiety and the improvements for you in
different areas of your life as a result.

Your work life

_____

_____

_____

_____

_____

Things around the home

_____

_____

_____

_____

_____

Your family life

_____

_____

_____

_____

_____

Your friendships

_____

_____

_____

_____

_____

Your social life

_____

_____

_____

_____

_____

How things have improved since the start of treatment

What things are you now doing that you were not doing when you were worrying extensively and anxious?

List here any changes you have noticed as signs of things improving for you:

_____

_____

_____

_____

_____

_____

_____

_____

_____

_____

_____

_____

_____

_____

_____

_____

List here the positive consequences of managing your worry and anxiety and the improvements for you in different areas of your life as a result.

Your work life

_____

_____

_____

_____

_____

Things around the home

_____

_____

_____

_____

_____

Your family life

_____

_____

_____

_____

_____

Your friendships

_____

_____

_____

_____

_____

Your social life

_____

_____

_____

_____

_____

My wellbeing action plan

Keeping check of my anxiety
Review date:
How have I been feeling this week/fortnight/month (delete as applicable)?   _____   _____   _____   _____   _____
Reading through early warning signs, have I had any that I am concerned about?   _____   _____   _____   _____   _____

Have I got any signs of:	Yes	No
• Hypothetical worries during the day that are hard to let go of:		
• Practical current worries that feel over-whelming to take any action about:		
• Avoiding things due to being anxious		
• Putting things off		
• Over-preparing for things		
• Seeking reassurance from friends, colleagues or loved ones		
• Feeling tense or other physical symptoms of anxiety		

Do I need to take any action now to manage my worry and anxiety?

_____

If I need to take action, what technique(s) helped before that I can use to help again?

_____

_____

_____

_____

_____

If so, what do I need to do and when am I going to do it?

_____

_____

_____

_____

_____

If things are going well, what is it that has been helping me?

_____

_____

_____

_____

_____

Keeping my worry management skills fresh

What are the key stages of the Worry Time technique?

_____

_____

_____

_____

_____

What are the key stages of the practical problem-solving technique?

_____

_____

_____

_____

_____

What are the key stages of progressive muscle relaxation?

_____

_____

_____

_____

_____

Date of my next review day:

_____

Put this on my calendar or phone so I will see it as a reminder.

My wellbeing action plan

Keeping check of my anxiety
Review date:
How have I been feeling this week/fortnight/month (delete as applicable)? _____ _____ _____ _____ _____
Reading through early warning signs, have I had any that I am concerned about? _____ _____ _____ _____ _____

Have I got any signs of:	Yes	No
• Hypothetical worries during the day that are hard to let go of:		
• Practical current worries that feel over-whelming to take any action about:		
• Avoiding things due to being anxious		
• Putting things off		
• Over-preparing for things		
• Seeking reassurance from friends, colleagues or loved ones		
• Feeling tense or other physical symptoms of anxiety		

Do I need to take any action now to manage my worry and anxiety?

_____

If I need to take action, what technique(s) helped before that I can use to help again?

_____

_____

_____

_____

_____

If so, what do I need to do and when am I going to do it?

_____

_____

_____

_____

_____

If things are going well, what is it that has been helping me?

_____

_____

_____

_____

_____

Keeping my worry management skills fresh

What are the key stages of the Worry Time technique?

_____

_____

_____

_____

_____

What are the key stages of the practical problem-solving technique?

_____

_____

_____

_____

_____

What are the key stages of progressive muscle relaxation?

_____

_____

_____

_____

_____

Date of my next review day:

_____

Put this on my calendar or phone so I will see it as a reminder.

My wellbeing action plan

Keeping check of my anxiety
Review date:
How have I been feeling this week/fortnight/month (delete as applicable)?
Reading through early warning signs, have I had any that I am concerned about?

Have I got any signs of:	Yes	No
• Hypothetical worries during the day that are hard to let go of:		
• Practical current worries that feel overwhelming to take any action about:		
• Avoiding things due to being anxious		
• Putting things off		
• Over-preparing for things		
• Seeking reassurance from friends, colleagues or loved ones		
• Feeling tense or other physical symptoms of anxiety		

Do I need to take any action now to manage my worry and anxiety?

_____

If I need to take action, what technique(s) helped before that I can use to help again?

_____

_____

_____

_____

_____

If so, what do I need to do and when am I going to do it?

_____

_____

_____

_____

_____

If things are going well, what is it that has been helping me?

_____

_____

_____

_____

_____

Keeping my worry management skills fresh

What are the key stages of the Worry Time technique?

_____

_____

_____

_____

_____

What are the key stages of the practical problem-solving technique?

_____

_____

_____

_____

_____

What are the key stages of progressive muscle relaxation?

_____

_____

_____

_____

_____

Date of my next review day:

_____

Put this on my calendar or phone so I will see it as a reminder.

My wellbeing action plan

Keeping check of my anxiety
Review date:
How have I been feeling this week/fortnight/month (delete as applicable)? _____ _____ _____ _____ _____
Reading through early warning signs, have I had any that I am concerned about? _____ _____ _____ _____ _____

Have I got any signs of:	Yes	No
• Hypothetical worries during the day that are hard to let go of:		
• Practical current worries that feel overwhelming to take any action about:		
• Avoiding things due to being anxious		
• Putting things off		
• Over-preparing for things		
• Seeking reassurance from friends, colleagues or loved ones		
• Feeling tense or other physical symptoms of anxiety		

Do I need to take any action now to manage my worry and anxiety?

_____

If I need to take action, what technique(s) helped before that I can use to help again?

_____

_____

_____

_____

_____

If so, what do I need to do and when am I going to do it?

_____

_____

_____

_____

_____

If things are going well, what is it that has been helping me?

_____

_____

_____

_____

_____

Keeping my worry management skills fresh

What are the key stages of the Worry Time technique?

_____

_____

_____

_____

_____

What are the key stages of the practical problem-solving technique?

_____

_____

_____

_____

_____

What are the key stages of progressive muscle relaxation?

_____

_____

_____

_____

_____

Date of my next review day:

_____

Put this on my calendar or phone so I will see it as a reminder.

Is there still anything you would like to work on?

If so what do you still want to do?

_____

_____

_____

_____

_____

How will you do it?

_____

_____

_____

_____

_____

When will you do it?

_____

_____

_____

_____

_____

Are there any resources you need to do it?

_____

_____

_____

_____

_____

What might get in the way of doing it and how can you overcome this?

_____

_____

_____

_____

_____

Is there still anything you would like to work on?

If so what do you still want to do?

_____

_____

_____

_____

_____

How will you do it?

_____

_____

_____

_____

_____

When will you do it?

_____

_____

_____

_____

_____

Are there any resources you need to do it?

_____

_____

_____

_____

_____

What might get in the way of doing it and how can you
overcome this?

_____

_____

_____

_____

_____

Is there still anything you would like to work on?

If so what do you still want to do?

_____

_____

_____

_____

_____

How will you do it?

_____

_____

_____

_____

_____

When will you do it?

_____

_____

_____

_____

_____

Are there any resources you need to do it?

_____

_____

_____

_____

_____

What might get in the way of doing it and how can you
overcome this?

_____

_____

_____

_____

_____

DEDICATIONS AND ACKNOWLEDGEMENTS

Marie:

This book is written in loving memory of my Mother, Bridget Chellingsworth, 1939–2008 and Father, John Montague Chellingsworth, 1937-2015. I would also like to dedicate it to all of the people with GAD I have had the privilege to work with over the years and from whom I have learned so much and to the practitioners that I have been lucky to train and supervise who make an invaluable difference to so many peoples' lives. Finally, thanks must go to the Editorial and Publishing team at Robinson who have been fantastic to work with and very patient!

Paul:

I would like to dedicate this book to my wife Paula, children Oliver, Ellis and Amélie, and family for all their love.

INDEX

A

aches and pains 26, 31, 64,
88, 125
adrenalin response 42, 64,
88, 101
useful purpose 99
antidepressants 40–1
anxiety
useful function 42
see also Generalized
Anxiety Disorder
(GAD); worries
apprehensive expectation
23, 35, 139–40, 141–2
avoidance behaviours 25,
26

B

back/joint problems 90
behavioural changes 26
avoidance behaviours
25, 26
over-preparation 25, 26
procrastination 25, 26,
34, 147
reassurance seeking 25,
26, 31, 145–6
benzodiazepines 39–40

breaking the pattern of worrying 27, 49, 76, 101
British Association
of Behavioural
and Cognitive
Psychotherapies
(BABCP) 38
buspirone 40

C

case studies
Graham 27, 30–2, 122–38
Sarah 29, 32–4, 138–51
causes of GAD 36
Cognitive Behavioural
Therapy (CBT) 1–2,
3, 38
CBT self-help (Low
Intensity CBT) 37–8
therapists 38, 119
compassion for yourself
100–1
concentration difficulties
25, 35, 124, 142

D

digestive disorders 26,
41–2, 88

distraction 49, 51, 66, 67, 71, 134
dry mouth 35

E

early warning signs 100, 101–2, 103, 104–6, 116
    ABC diagram 105, 185
edge, feeling on 24, 35, 125

F

family and friends, support from 11, 118
family history and GAD 36
fight, flight, freeze or flop response 64, 88
financial worries 48, 140, 146–7, 149–50

G

Generalized Anxiety Disorder (GAD)
    causes 36
    questions about 35–43
    signs and symptoms 35
    top tips 44–5, 116–17
    treatments 36–41, 42
    understanding 23–7
    website information 35–6
goals
    further work on 114–15, 234–9
    rating 18–21, 163–71
    re-rating 96–7
    setting 15–18, 154–62
    specific to you 18
    worksheets 16–18, 19–21, 114–15, 154–71, 234–9

GPs 9, 11, 37–8, 90, 95, 127–8

H

headaches 26, 30, 31, 64, 88, 126, 127
health worries 48
help and support, getting 9–11, 117–19
hypothetical worries 47, 48, 50, 60, 61, 65–6, 69–70, 101, 106, 129, 130
    worksheets 75, 186–9

I

Improving Access to Psychological Therapies (IAPT) services 9, 119
irritability 25, 141
Irritable Bowel Syndrome (IBS) 41–2

J

jaw and teeth clenching 134
job worries 48, 140–1

M

managing your worries *see* problem solving technique; Progressive Muscle Relaxation (PGMR); Worry Time
medication 38–41
    antidepressants 40–1
    benzodiazepines 39–40
    buspirone 40
    discontinuation 39, 40, 41
mood fluctuations, normal 99

motivating yourself 13–14,
    21–2, 106–9
  exercises 14
  worksheets 107–9,
    206–17
muscle spasms 90
muscular tension 24, 25,
    26, 31, 45, 46, 64, 88,
    89, 125
  see also Progressive
    Muscle Relaxation
    (PGMR)

N

National Institute of Health
    and Care Excellence
    (NICE) 1–2, 36, 37
night, worrying at 44, 55, 70
normal and helpful
    worrying 43, 44, 102,
    150

O

over-preparation 25, 26

P

palpitations 35
penguin experiment 51–2
physical problems *see* signs
    and symptoms
pins and needles 26
practical worries 47–8,
    49–50, 60, 61, 77, 101,
    106, 129, 146–7
  see also problem solving
problem solving 44, 63, 65,
    77–83, 77–87, 146–9
problem solving technique
  carrying out your chosen
    solution 81

constructing a realistic
    plan 80–1
  how long to use the
    technique 83
  reviewing the outcome 82
  solutions, identifying
    78–9
  solutions, ranking 79–80
  solutions, strengths and
    weaknesses of 79
  worksheets 84–7, 190–205
  writing down your
    practical worry 78
procrastination 25, 26, 34, 147
Progressive Muscle
    Relaxation (PGMR)
    45, 64–5, 83, 88–95
  GP approval 90, 91
  how often to practice
    89–90, 94–5, 131
  pre-existing health
    conditions and 90
  set time for 90
  technique 91–4
Psychological Wellbeing
    Practitioners (PWPs)
    9, 37

R

reassurance seeking 25, 26,
    31, 145–6
recovery stories 2
  Graham 122–38
  Sarah 138–51
red flag symptoms *see* early
    warning signs
refocusing your mind on
    the present moment
    44, 45, 62, 70–2, 74,
    75, 117, 135–6

relapse
  breaking the pattern of
      worrying 101
  compassion for yourself
      100–1
  definition 102–3
  early warning signs 100,
      101–2, 103, 104–6,
      116
  fear of 98–9
  lapse, temporary 102
  relapse-prevention toolkit
      100, 101–2, 117,
      119–20
repetitive worries 56, 69–70

S

Selective Noradrenalin
      Reuptake Inhibitors
      (SNRIs) 40
Selective Serotonin
      Reuptake Inhibitors
      (SSRIs) 40–1
serotonin 40
Sertraline 41
signs and symptoms 35
  aches and pains 26, 31,
      64, 88, 125, 139–40,
      141–2
  apprehensive expectation
      23, 35
  concentration difficulties
      25, 35, 124, 142
  disturbed sleep 26, 44,
      55, 88
  dry mouth 35
  early warning signs 100,
      101–2, 103, 104–6
  edge, feeling on 24, 35,
      125

  headaches 26, 30, 31, 64,
      88, 126, 127
  irritability 25, 141
  jaw and teeth clenching
      134
  palpitations 35
  pins and needles 26
  sweating 26
  tension 24, 25, 26, 31, 45,
      46, 64, 88, 89, 125
  tiredness and exhaustion
      26, 125, 126
  sleep, disturbed 26, 44,
      55, 88
  stomach upsets 26, 41–2,
      88
  sweating 26

T

tension 24, 25, 26, 31, 45,
      46, 64, 88, 89, 125
therapists 38, 119, 128, 129,
      130–1, 134–5, 144–5,
      147
thought suppression 51, 53,
      66, 67
tiredness and exhaustion
      26, 125, 126
top tips 44–5, 116–17

V

vicious cycle of worry and
      anxiety 24, 25–6, 43,
      46, 66, 76, 88, 100,
      102–3, 106
  breaking into 27, 49, 76,
      101
  diagram 28
visualisation 14

W

wellbeing action plan 101–
2, 104, 109–13, 116
worksheets 110–13,
218–33
worries
classifying 46–8, 49–50,
56, 60, 129–30
hypothetical worries 47,
48, 50, 60, 61, 65–6,
69–70, 101, 106, 129,
130
interventions *see* problem
solving technique;
Progressive Muscle
Relaxation (PGMR);
Worry Time
normal and helpful
worrying 43, 44, 102,
150
practical worries 47–8,
49–50, 60, 61, 77, 101,
106, 129, 146–7
ranking worries 54
repetitive worries 56,
69–70
suppression 51, 66
top tips for dealing with
44–5, 116–17

vicious cycle of worry and
anxiety 24, 25–6, 43,
46, 66, 76, 88, 100,
102–3, 106
writing worries down 43,
44, 54–7, 69–70, 78
Worry Diary 54, 55, 57,
58–9, 129–30, 132–3
reflecting on 60–1, 130
worksheets 58–9, 172–83
Worry Time 44, 45, 62, 65–
76, 83, 134–7, 146
how long to use the
technique 76
planning your Worry
Time 68
reflecting afterwards 73–4
refocusing your mind on
the present moment
70–2, 74, 75
technique 65–74
worksheets 75, 186–9
Worry List 72–3
writing
in the book 12
a letter to yourself 120
writing worries down 43,
44, 54–7, 69–70, 78

How to Beat Panic Disorder
One Step at a Time

Using evidence-based low-intensity CBT

Paul Farrand and Marie Chellingsworth

ISBN: 978-1-47210-884-5 (paperback)

ISBN: 978-1-47211-343-6 (ebook)

Price: £7.99

book is the perfect resource for helping you to beat panic
order, either by yourself or in conjunction with the support
an IAPT service. It is written in a friendly, engaging (and
jargon-free!) style and encourages interactive reading through
tables, illustrations and worksheets. Real-life case studies illustrate the use of each intervention and demonstrate how you can
work through your moments of panic. You will learn effective
techniques from Cognitive Behavioural Therapy that have been
shown to work for people with panic disorder.

How to Beat Depression
One Step at a Time

Using evidence-based low-intensity CBT

Marie Chellingsworth and Paul Farrand

ISBN: 978-1-47210-883-8 (paperback)

ISBN: 978-1-47211-342-9 (ebook)

Price: £7.99

This book is the perfect resource for helping yo͏͏ [   ]
mood and depression, either by yourself or in conjun[   ]
with the support of an IAPT service. It is written in a friendly,
engaging (and jargon-free!) style and encourages interactive
reading through tables, illustrations and worksheets. Real-
life case studies illustrate the use of each intervention and
demonstrate how you can work through your depression. The
book draws on a therapeutic approach known as Behavioural
Activation, which has been recommended as an effective
method of treating depression.